SOPH
'BRINGING S

*A series of books which bring modern
spiritual ideas into life—for
practical use in everyday life.*

The Journey Continues . . .

The Journey Continues...

Finding a New Relationship to Death

Dr Gilbert Childs
with Sylvia Childs

SOPHIA BOOKS
Rudolf Steiner Press
London

Sophia Books
Rudolf Steiner Press
51 Queen Caroline Street
London W6 9QL

First published by Sophia Books 1998
(Sophia Books is an imprint of Rudolf Steiner Press)

A catalogue record for this book is available from
the British Library

ISBN 1 85584 086 3

Cover by Andrew Morgan, incorporating a painting by Anne Stockton
Typeset by DP Photosetting, Aylesbury, Bucks
Printed and bound in Great Britain by
Cromwell Press Limited, Trowbridge, Wiltshire

To Sylvia Childs
⋆ 29 November 1939   † 29 August 1996

I was united with you.
So remain united in me.
Together we shall speak
The speech of eternal being.
Together we shall act
Where the results of our deeds are at work.
Together we shall weave in spirit,
Where human thought is woven,
In the Word of eternal thought.

Rudolf Steiner

Contents

Introduction

We may not ourselves suffer bereavement, but we are certain to experience that which we know as death. The suggestion that this inevitable event should not be regarded with the usual fear and dread may give joy to some, relief to others and, I hope, consolation to everyone. This little book will deal with only the basic features of this mysterious event, revealing them in a light that is at once cautionary and comforting.

There are three basic teachings that the Austrian scientist and philosopher Dr Rudolf Steiner brought together under the name of Anthroposophy, the science of the spirit which he sought to establish during the first quarter of the twentieth century. These are: 1) human beings are firstly spiritual in nature, and only secondly beings of matter; 2) the realities of reincarnation are shown in individual and public history, and 3) the truth of the workings of karma or self-created destiny can be discerned in our lives. I have attempted to explore all three from various angles, and have also looked at the very real comparisons between death and its 'small brother' sleep, and the issues that oblige groups of people to descend to Earth at the same time, there to seek one another out and re-link their common destinies.

Unreserved acknowledgement is given to Rudolf Steiner, some of whose beautiful and inspiring meditations chosen from the great treasury he left us are to be found sprinkled throughout the text. When the time came for him to pass through the gate of death he folded his hands over his breast and closed his eyes before drawing his final breath, in full and serene awareness of both material and spiritual worlds.

1.

Our Spiritual Roots

All things alive throughout the Universe
Live but in bringing forth within them
The seed of a new life.
So too the soul of Man is given up
To ageing and to death,
Only that deathless he may ripen
To ever newly resurrected life.[1]

Worlds seen and unseen

Our ancestors knew very well that they were inhabitants of two worlds—the heavenly and the earthly. Mythologies of every race, nation or people trace their origins to the heavenly worlds, the unseen worlds, the *spiritual* worlds. It is often difficult for us, surrounded as we are by a world that is solid and *material*, to imagine what our forefathers experienced in their daily lives, and how they viewed nature and the universe. As they were aware of both worlds, they treated them as equally real. The whole history of mankind is characterized by the progression from a state of extensive vision into the spiritual world combined with limited awareness of the sensible world to limited awareness of the supersensible world but extensive clarity of vision and understanding of the material world.

A widespread belief common among the far ancestors of the peoples of virtually the whole world was that the dead returned to their forefathers, and this has survived among the so-called undeveloped peoples where tribalism still exists. The term 'ancestor-worship' is not really appropriate, because it represents rather a mood of reverence and respect, of love and veneration, and may best be regarded as respectful behaviour involving the dead customary in all civilizations, both ancient and modern. Interestingly enough, many old-established cultures have one word for worshipping their deities and quite another for showing veneration for their forebears, and it is noteworthy that the Zulu word for ancestor veneration, namely, *ukuthetha*, means literally 'speaking with', and that tells its own story. So our forebears really did know that the dead, although absent in body, were nevertheless present in spirit, and they sought by all manner of means to communicate with them, consult with them, and seek their guidance. The literature concerning all kinds of such customs, traditions and beliefs, although somewhat garbled and distorted over time, is immense. But in spite of the feeling of authenticity common to them all, many people refuse to accept the proposition that there is a life beyond death. Rudolf Steiner agreed with our forebears:

> If we manage to keep alive and awake the memory of our dear ones who have died; if we can keep our thoughts of them constantly and vividly before us during waking life, then the memory-pictures we lovingly carry within us will enable the dead to have an influence upon our world, to pour their will into it, so that their will lives on in the will of those who are still alive. If we manage continually to re-enliven our memory of the dead during our waking life, this will also accompany us and have an effect during sleep. The dead experience and feel what

we bring into the spiritual world every time we fall asleep. We can enable the dead, when we sleep, to unite their perception with the images of them we faithfully preserve and guard. So we can learn truly to live with those who have died.[2]

Historians agree that history proper grew out of mythology, and that every culture has its own system of beliefs in this respect. Difficult as it may frequently be to interpret the various Creation stories, references to spiritual beings, gods, heroes and suchlike, every effort should be made to explain them in their own terms. Various accounts have been put forward to explain the universal belief on the part of all early peoples in superhuman, supersensible beings whose main attributes were limitless power and knowledge. Anthropologists and sociologists generally uphold the notion of *animism*, put forward in an attempt to explain in rational terms why primitive tribes attribute soul-spiritual qualities to natural objects and phenomena. The seemingly fictional element present in mythological explanations of pre-historical times and events is widely regarded as amounting to mere 'fairy-tales', and this has led to the dangerously misleading notion that myths and legends are mere inventions of the primitive mind, which they are not.

Undoubtedly there has been, over the centuries, a constant garbling of the original imaginations and inspirations contained in all myths and legends because pre-literate civilizations were bound to rely on their being passed on by word of mouth. The mistake is frequently made of thinking that merely because our ancestors could not express themselves in intellectual ways that they were unintelligent. Allegorical, metaphorical or other explanations should be attempted only with great caution, for there invariably exists the tendency of many scholars to read back into the past their modern ways of looking at things. Moreover, it is equally misleading to try to rationalize that which was not a work of reason in the first place.

The rise of materialism

The struggle for some kind of reconciliation between religion and science is, in effect, a battle for compromise involving spirit and matter. The two sets of beliefs have been at odds for a long time. Theology, as the medieval queen of the sciences, was displaced by science 'proper' in the nineteenth century with the rise of Darwinism, which has been unstoppable ever since. This has resulted in a new religion—that of materialism in various forms—now becoming firmly established.

This was inevitable with the onset of the Age of Reason, the Industrial Revolution and so on, for the Churches had no answer. This is understandable enough, for there was a sea-change in thinking habits by the ordinary public, who could see with their own eyes that science 'worked', whereas their prayers never seemed to be answered. In desperation, organized religion resorted to dogma and doctrine, from papal infallibility to religious fundamentalism. There had long been no real understanding of 'spirit', and there was no defence against the all-conquering progress of materialism. But religious or moral teachings alone are effective only where there is ignorance, and ignorance of the worlds of the spirit was characteristic of the whole period.

This being so, the decline of organized religion in the so-called civilized world has been relentless. What was desperately needed, in terms of genuine progress, was the appearance of a scientist who could investigate the world of spirit as well as matter, and as if by cue Rudolf Steiner (1861–1925) appeared on the scene. In 1902 he publicly declared his life's aim to be the founding of new methods of spiritual research on a scientific basis. Trained as a scientist, and familiar with its methodologies, he applied the same rigour associated with these to his own investigations in the unseen, supersensible worlds. He was no woolly-minded mystic or visionary, but strove energetically to demonstrate the truly complementary character of both sensory and supersensory realms. That he was to a considerable extent successful in his endeavours is evidenced by the practical nature of those indications he gave, particularly in the areas of education, medicine, agriculture, architecture and the arts, as well as the social sciences in general, which have been taken up, extended and developed.

He consistently showed that spiritual truths, and knowledge supersensibly acquired, are in complete and necessary agreement with the knowledge that can be gained from the world of the senses, that is to say, by scientific methodologies applicable to both worlds. Reflection will show that this cannot be otherwise: if to the 'half-reality' of sense-perception is added the complementary 'half-reality' of supersensible perception, the result can only be understanding of absolute, total reality. The notion that knowledge of both seen and unseen worlds be brought together as Steiner intended makes perfect sense, and the stubborn refusal of orthodox science even to examine the tenets of spiritual science is both unreasonable and unfortunate. During his lifetime he met unwarranted and vehement opposition to his findings from the orthodox sector, which has for the most part persisted since.

The ordered universe

It is a matter for debate whether our inclination to think logically arose from humanity's long acquaintance with nature and its laws, or vice versa. The fact is that we do think logically, and we cultivate this ability because it is seen to work when applied to practical affairs. All science seemingly relies on the twin factors of cause and effect, and its overriding value lies in the fact that it has confirmed order in the whole of Creation. The Greek word *kosmos* cannot only mean 'world' or 'universe' (and this directly on account of its 'perfect arrangement'), but also means 'order' as against *chaos*, the Greek word meaning disorder or confusion.

Since natural law and order is seen to prevail in the material world, then we may safely conclude that it exists also in the spiritual world. The cause and effect of every event must, *in terms of the Whole*, be co-existent, inter-dependent and complementary. Our very word 'universe' derives from the Latin word for 'entire' or 'whole', and has its origin in the meaning of 'turning towards', and the spiritual and material worlds turn towards each other in every conceivable way. The implications are inescapable: we are not only 'in' the universe, we are also 'of' it in every sense. We are not only earthly in nature, we are also heavenly; we are indeed *spiritual* as well as *material* beings.

We know from our own experience that there are things which are incapable of being grasped by any of the so-called five senses but which nonetheless possess an undeniable reality. These include our feelings, thoughts and ideas, our unrealized dreams, aims and goals, our moral standards, our hopes and fears. All these make up our own inner, private world existing in contradistinction to the outer world, which is relatively public and accessible to others; and interaction between the two makes up our everyday experiences. Everything that belongs to our mental and emotional faculties is invisible and intangible. Nevertheless, they possess reality, and therefore can be said to consist, if not of an actual substance, then of something *substantial*. We know that material substances come from a material world; therefore it is reasonable to assert that our very real substantiality—in terms of personality characteristics and individual traits—also maintain its existence in an actual, if necessarily invisible and intangible, world.

These attributes may be said to exist in qualities of 'soul' or 'spirit'. People talk of body, soul and spirit, body, mind and spirit, mind and body, body and soul and so on according to how they regard themselves as being made up. However one expresses it, if our body of mineral substances derives from the world of matter, our 'body' of soul-spiritual, or 'mental-emotional' substantiality must derive from an *im*material world. We are indeed citizens of two worlds—one composed of matter and the other of spirit.

What is spirit? What is matter?

It is impossible to answer such questions as these in any way that is fixed, definitive and final. Materialistic scientists argue that we consist of body only, claiming that all we experience in terms of thoughts and feelings arise by reason of our purely physiological processes, our bodily natures. Consciousness, according to them, is produced by mechanisms associated with our brain and nervous system on the general principle: no brain, no consciousness; no nerves, no sense-impressions. Common everyday experience, based on the notion of our inner and outer worlds touched on just now, suggests that human nature consists of at least two principles, if not three. Scientific orthodoxy claims that living organisms arose more or less by chance from a kind of 'primeval soup', and that we human beings are the consequences of this haphazard event. Briefly, it teaches that what is living arose from that which was lifeless and inert, not the other way round. This is the standpoint of modern orthodox science, and is widely regarded as unchallengeable. However, the geologist Walther Cloos argues that everything which is inert and lifeless in terms of the mineral world has been *previously alive*, or derived from that which had once been living.[3]

Matter is something that is capable of being perceived by one or more of our sense-organs. Now our eyes, ears, nose, taste-buds and such organs are themselves composed of matter, so it is logical and correct to presume that they are capable of perceiving only that which is also constituted of matter. Such immaterial realities as thoughts and feelings are not perceived *directly* by the five senses, belonging as they do to the unseen worlds of soul and spirit, yet their reality cannot be denied.

Some attributes of spirit

'God is a Spirit' (John 4:24), and this notion ties in very neatly with the attribute of creativity. For creativity to manifest itself the necessary power to do so must be present. Modern science finds it impossible to describe just how life arises. To say simply that it does arise, or arises of itself, is tantamount to saying that it comes out of nothing. The problem is that life itself cannot be seen, but can only be detected in the way it is able to work through, and by means of, matter. Spirit is pure being, creative and dynamic; matter is created and static. Spirit is the active principle at all times and in all circumstances, and matter that which is acted *upon*. Modern materialistic scientists scorn the notion that the unseen gives rise to that which can be seen, and never admit that the bodily sense-organs we all rely upon so heavily are themselves due to the activity of immaterial agencies.

If we are made in the image of God then we must be spiritual in nature. This is what our ancestors believed— indeed, must have *known*—and this belief is still being perpetuated in terms of religion. The very word derives from the Latin *religare* which means 'to bind back', and all religious people are, consciously or unconsciously, seeking to *return* to God, 'heaven', 'Universal All', or similar, from which they have somehow become alienated. A majority of people sense that there is a Power, vastly superior in every way to ourselves, which seems to be eminently capable of preserving the 'order' that we see all around us. If the 'world order' is thus perfectly arranged in the sense of *kosmos*, it stands to reason that the Creator must have possessed the attributes of perfection, or at least the power to order things to perfection.

Orthodox scientists invariably argue that our waking consciousness is a phenomenon somehow 'produced' by the brain, denying that this brain is simply and purely the *organ* of consciousness. Attempts to explain other states of consciousness we experience every day and night of the week, namely, dream consciousness and sleep conscious-ness, remain unconvincing. Memory-pictures and processes of recall in general are still a mystery to them, yet spiritual science explains them clearly and convincingly.[4] The whole notion of sense-free thinking, which Steiner proved to be perfectly possible, remains foreign to ortho-dox science.[5]

And what of immortality?

Many people, when asked, 'Do you believe in life after death?' reply that they do. Further questioning often reveals simply how much muddle and misconception surround the whole matter. It is a highly personal one in any case, but surveys tend to show that most people harbour a vague notion that the 'soul' is somehow immortal but cannot always say clearly in what way. Generally speaking, their position reflects the uneasy relationship that has existed in the past between religion and science, 'belief' and 'knowledge', and has made it impossible, for example, to prove or disprove the existence of God, for religion has rested on belief rather than certainty. Some people would like to imagine that there is a kind of existence after death, perhaps that they go on 'living' in the memories of surviving friends and relations, but this is small consolation, for such remembrance is bound to fade out after two or three generations.

There is much talk of deathlessness, but very little of its companion, which is birthlessness or 'unbornness'. Religious teaching maintains that the soul continues to exist after death, but details given of such existence are very scanty. The problem is an old one. For example, the Greek Church Father Origen (185–254) actually preached the 'pre-existence of the soul', whereas the Latin Church Father St Jerome (*c.* 340–420) taught that 'God is daily fashioning souls'. The apostle Paul maintained that human beings have a threefold nature, namely, spirit, soul and body. What many people today denote by 'soul' is our spirit and soul natures taken together in combination. The confusion arises because we cannot normally see or touch these entities. In everyday speech, distinctions between soul and spirit are not always made, the two terms being used interchangeably, and it is common to speak of 'body, mind and spirit' without mentioning the word 'soul'. For present purposes, we contend that the soul proper arises from the interaction between our spiritual nature and our bodily nature, and this will be discussed in the following chapter. Perhaps we shall come to see that death signifies a change in our consciousness and another kind of existence, and that immortality consists in our retaining that consciousness, whatever changes we are obliged to undergo in whatever circumstances, whether in the earthly or the heavenly worlds.

2.

The Complexities of Human Nature

You, yourself,
As a person of knowing, feeling and will,
You are the riddle of the world.
What in the world is concealed
Grows manifest in you.
It becomes light in your spirit,
It becomes warmth in your soul.
Your breathing binds your body's life
To worlds of soul and realms of spirit.
It leads you into the domain of matter,
So that you may find your true humanity.
It directs you towards the spirit,
So that you do not lose yourself.[1]

What is our true nature?

It is an everyday human experience to be aware both of our visible nature (our body) and of our unseen nature—our thoughts, emotions, impulses of will and suchlike. This gives rise to the assumption or belief that we human beings have a spiritual nature generally referred to as the *soul*, and a material nature called the *body*. Modern science, however, has succeeded in leaving us with the widespread notion that we consist of body only, our psychological attributes arising as incidental to its various processes and functions.

A more refined model of the human being is the threefold one of body, soul and spirit, given by the apostle

Paul in a letter to the Thessalonians: 'May God himself, the God of peace, make you holy in every part, and keep you sound in spirit, soul and body' (1 Thessalonians 5:23). That we possess a physical-material organization is not in doubt, but many people find it difficult to distinguish between soul and spirit, for they both give rise to inner experiences, and confusion concerning the two principles is common. Rudolf Steiner made the differences crystal clear:

Through his* body he is related to the objects which present themselves to his senses from without. The materials from the outer world compose this body of his; and the forces of the outer world work also in it. And just as he observes the things of the outer world with his senses, so can he also observe his own bodily existence. But it is impossible to observe his soul existence in the same way. Everything in me which is bodily process can be perceived with bodily eyes. My likes and dislikes, my joy and pain, neither I nor anyone else can perceive with bodily senses. The region of the soul is one which is inaccessible to bodily perception. The bodily existence of man is manifest to all eyes; the soul existence he carries within himself as his world. Through the spirit, however, the outer world is revealed to him in a higher way. The mysteries of the outer world, indeed, unveil themselves in his inner being; but he steps in spirit out of himself and lets the things speak for themselves, about that which has significance not for him, but for them. The human being looks up at the starry heavens, the delight his soul experiences belongs to him; the eternal laws of the stars

---

* Rudolf Steiner is making reference to a *human being*, a *person*—man or woman—in this and other quotations from his works.

which he comprehends in thought, in spirit, belong not to him but the stars themselves.

Thus, the human being is citizen of three worlds. Through his body he belongs to the world which he perceives through his body; through his soul he constructs for himself his own world; through his spirit a world reveals itself to him which is exalted above all the others.[2]

Such a description may seem at first sight to be too simplistic, but it is carefully worded and repays thought and reflection. Our physical body obviously consists of material from the outer mineral world; therefore, our bodily senses are themselves composed of matter. From this it follows that *only* that which is physical-material in nature is perceivable by these senses. Of course we are able to 'sense' what is going on in the mind or emotions of another person—but this can only be done indirectly, by interpreting the tone of voice, gestures and similar signals involving body language and other means of non-verbal communication.

Just as our body consists of substance from the material world, so our soul comprises 'soul substance'. We all have differing tastes, likes and dislikes, varying joys and sorrows, and feelings of pleasure and pain. All these human attributes which characterize our life of *feeling* are therefore *universal* in character; every word in one language is capable of being expressed in all other languages, and of making sense. It is therefore perfectly reasonable to contend that there exists a universally common soul substance from which our souls are composed, just as there is material substance which constitutes our physical-material bodies.

A materialist would argue that all our emotions arise from our bodily nature and, as all human beings are constituted in similar fashion, such universality and similarity in terms of our general behaviour is to be expected. In this connection it could be difficult for the holders of such a notion to explain how the higher human qualities, such as altruism, self-sacrifice, refined moral standards and suchlike, arise from purely bodily processes. The kind of universal quality that involves our *feelings* in the case of our soul allows our thoughts, opinions and viewpoints, which are essentially the result of spiritual activity, to be understood by everyone.

The soul links body and spirit

The essential threefolding of human nature was put with admirable conciseness by Irenaeus (*c.* 130–*c.* 200), one of the early Church Fathers, as follows: 'The perfect man consists of these three: flesh, soul and spirit. One of these saves and fashions—that is, the spirit. Another is united and formed—that is, the flesh; while that which lies between the two is the soul, which sometimes follows the spirit and is raised by it, but at other times sympathizes with the flesh and is drawn into it by earthly passions.' Here we can see the intermediary character of the soul, which dwells in the body and is sustained by it. In similar fashion the spirit abides in and is nurtured by the soul. Thus our 'lower nature', represented by the body, is in a position to influence the soul. The spirit, which we may regard with justification as representing our 'higher self', is also in direct connection with the soul. Thus the spirit, the originator of all our higher thoughts, ideals and so on, is able to bring these about by first inspiring our soul towards bodily action, in the manner of deeds and accomplishments in the world.

The body is the servant of the soul during our lifetime. In

its function as intermediary between spirit and body, the soul is perfectly placed for translating the experiences of the senses into *inner* experiences. The spirit cannot experience matter directly, but is able to receive through the soul our harvest of earthly experience. After the body dies, the soul too eventually fades away during the period after death. However, we shall see that its essential character survives as a kind of 'extract' that forms the basis of the new soul of the next incarnation.

Spirit, soul and body in action

Our *thinking* faculty is creative and universal in character, and concepts employed in one language are similarly translatable into others. Thinking is a spiritual activity, which enables us to formulate our own ideas, and grasp with our powers of understanding the thoughts of others. Thoughts are actual entities; we are motivated to employ all our mental powers in observation and research, reasoning and analysis to reach the objectives set by our ideals. In turn our notions prompt discussion and debate, argument and counter-argument, and other processes which result in the refinement of ideas and the possibility, feasibility or certainty of their successful implementation in society, industry and commerce—indeed, whatever their application in world affairs. So much for the activity of our *heads*. But ideas, theories and feasibility studies are useless if they are not realized in our deeds, our acts of will.

As Pascal observed, the heart has reasons that reason doesn't know, but at the same time we realize that knowledge acquired by reason of our *hearts* is just as important as that acquired through our heads. That is to say, our *feelings* often inspire us to action, so that our ideals, and those of others, may be fulfilled and achieved. Our feelings and emotions sway back and forth, our likes and dislikes wax and wane, our joys and woes come and go. Such experiences seem to be more immediate and closer to us than our thoughts, which usually take on a more detached or distant character. We are of course speaking of the general area of the *soul*, the bearer of all our sympathies and antipathies, and arguably the primary source of incentive for action. Our inner lives are for the most part dominated by our life of soul, for if we don't *feel* attracted by a certain idea it is often dismissed from our minds—and it is usually unhappy people who carry out actions they do not feel like doing.

The whole business of *action* has to do with *will-power*, and deeds usually involve the limbs, the employment of the strength and capabilities of the *body*. Obviously, the mere action of thinking, which is confined to our head, cannot of its own power get things done in the outer world, and the same can be said of our feelings. Both faculties have to be expressed or implemented by means of our limbs, and in many cases their extension in the shape of tools and mechanical aids of all kinds. This is how the human *spirit*, which is totally powerless on the physical plane, achieves its aims and intentions, and brings about changes in the outside world. Obviously, the consequences of such actions and events which have been brought about by human endeavour are subject to appraisal and other kinds of 'feedback', so that the spirit may in turn inspire further action of whatever kind deemed appropriate.

Our fourfold constitution

It is possible to present an elegant and valid model of the human being as fourfold, in addition to, or as replacement of, the threefold one just outlined. This one is based on notions that were well known among the ancient Greeks, centuries before the establishment of Christianity. Greek science saw nature in fourfold terms: Fire, Air, Water and Earth. To them everything that was connected with heat and high temperatures was represented by the element of Fire, and this was characterized for instance by the heat of the sun, and the warmth of our blood, as well as ordinary flames. The element of Air was associated with everything that is gaseous in character and constitution, just as everything that manifested a fluid nature was categorized as Water, whether the liquid be actual water, wine, juices—whatever flowed was Water. The element of Earth stood for all substances that were solid, and the qualities of resistance, form and weight associated with such materials or objects identified them as earthly. Apart from rocks, stones and the more obvious solid stuff, material such as bones, shells, wood and most metals were similarly classified.

All this seems sensible enough for the times, and of course the general principles still hold. Looking around us in the world, we are soon able to observe that there are comparatively inert and lifeless substances everywhere, such as soil, stones and minerals, which do not change their outward natures to any appreciable degree. Sandstone can be hammered and ground into small particles, which still retain their hardness and other 'earthly' qualities. Such substances, which are classified in terms of chemical elements by modern science, interact with one another in a purely chemical fashion, or by the agency of such physical forces as frost, heat, friction and so on. They may change their chemical formulae and even their nature according to the Greek way of classification, into liquids, gases or even fire. Any kind of change or metamorphosis results from purely chemical or physical action.

Our etheric or 'life' body

It is not difficult to discern the association between Earth in the Greek sense and our physical-material principle, for our physical body obtains its constitution in mineral and chemical terms from the very earth beneath our feet. These material substances are taken up by that which exhibits all the qualities we associate with *life*, and which pre-scientific natural philosophy explained with the term *élan vital* or 'vital force'. This was considered quite rightly to account for the difference between inert chemical substances and the way they appeared in the plants which had extracted them from the earth with the help of light and heat, air and moisture. Thus it could be seen that the agency of all or some of the other three 'elements'—namely, Fire, Air, and Water—working together were needed for this life-process, itself invisible and undetectable by any of our senses, to operate. When circumstances are present which allow life-processes to function, the end result is seen to appear not only in *space* but also through *time*.

This life-principle, thus seen to be at work in all living beings, whether plant, animal or human, is well known to spiritual science, and is often called the etheric body. It was sometimes referred to more graphically by Rudolf Steiner as the 'formative-forces body'. An immediately discernible characteristic of this etheric body is that it has strong con- nections with time, for it is only over a period of time that organisms build, form, organize, bring to maturity and make preparations to ensure the continuation of its species by means of some kind of propagation process. A major characteristic of life in all its forms is *rhythm*, and this is one of the hallmarks of etheric forces which manifest in the whole of nature, with its rhythms of emergence, growth, decay and departure or 'death'.

The etheric forces are always associated with the presence of water, and it is well known that the human being is composed mostly of water—hence the medium is there for the functions of healing, repair and regeneration of the cells. The etheric body is therefore responsible for providing the patterns of growth, shape, form and function of the bodily organs, including of course those of reproduction. Although every seven years every cell in the body is renewed, each organ during this process retains its nature and constitution, which is faithfully preserved by the etheric organization. In due course, this life-body is observed to depart from the physical-material entity that it has helped to organize and construct, and this event is commonly known as *death*.

The plant kingdom leads as it were a life of permanent sleep, as no tree, shrub, plant or vegetable is conscious in the way that animals and humans are. They do not possess sense organs and a nervous system as sentient creatures do, and as a rule they have no means of locomotion. Any movements discernible in the leaves, flowers and fruit of plants and trees are invariably due to outside stimuli, and are utterly mechanical, and not carried out as the result of wish or choice.

Our astral or 'consciousness' body

According to ancient tradition, our 'consciousness-system' was referred to as our 'astral' or 'starry' body, because there are certain definite connections with the starry worlds—

and this has been confirmed by Rudolf Steiner.[3] The riddle of consciousness remains a riddle to modern science, and philosophers are faced with the problem of consciousness having to examine itself, a feat that is not easy to accomplish. When most people think of consciousness, they usually 'have in mind' our ordinary waking consciousness—that is to say, our *thinking* consciousness. We all experience the endless flow of sense-impressions which fills most of our waking life. Impressions with which we are familiar pose no problem, but when we meet new or unfamiliar ones we must learn how to integrate them into our already established patterns of thinking in the form of concepts, ideas and so forth. Thus we each build our own private world of thought which we inhabit and know so well.

Our normal waking consciousness involves to a great extent a continuous stream of impressions that pour in via our sense organs—sight, hearing, smell, taste and touch—upon which we rely so heavily as we go about our daily tasks and other activities. But even when we are resting, perhaps with our eyes closed and receiving barely a single sense-impression, our mind—our consciousness—is occupied with thoughts and ideas, memories and reflections, hopes and fears, plans for the immediate and distant future, and so on.

Our mental life is usually active all the time we are awake; rarely, if ever, is our mind a total blank. Earlier, reference was made to our 'consciousness-system' or sentient organization as a 'body', but this does not of course refer to anything solid or material. Our sense organs, however, and the central nervous system and brain which are connected with them, are obviously constituted of living tissues which do consist of matter. Although we cannot see or touch thoughts and feelings, the fact that they do comprise an organized structure justifies the use of the term 'body'.

That little word 'I'

Animals possess conscious awareness, whereas human beings possess self-conscious awareness. We see ourselves, and experience ourselves, as totally individual in nature and character, and we act accordingly. We each possess a definite sense of selfhood, of being separate from our surroundings. This consciousness of self is readily confirmed by our employment of the personal pronoun 'I', a word that cannot be used by anyone else to mean the same thing. We all see ourselves over against everything that is not enclosed within our skin as a kind of 'not-self', and this enables us to become aware of ourselves as subject and the rest of Creation as object. The expression 'I' represents our *ego*, that which imparts the feeling of selfhood or identity familiar to each one of us, and which is the agent by which we make all our decisions and by which we direct our lives. We all feel that we are 'masters of our fate, and captains of our soul'— within certain constraints—and it is our life experiences which do much to define these and allow for them.

It is easy to jump to the conclusion that animals have egos too. But a moment's reflection will show that while it cannot be denied that animals, unlike plants and minerals, are conscious, it cannot be said that they are *self*-conscious. They have an individuality of sorts, and they also exhibit a kind of instinctive social life, but their appearance and their essential nature conform to that of the whole species to which they belong. What we have discussed so far may be expressed in a simple table:

Kingdom of Nature	Principles sustained
Mineral	Physical
Plant	Physical, Etheric
Animal	Physical, Etheric, Astral
Human	Physical, Etheric, Astral, Ego

Waking, dreaming and sleeping

We are so preoccupied with our sharp and clear daytime awareness that we scarcely stop to reflect on our two other states, dreaming and sleeping, yet they are equally important to our overall well-being. We are all familiar with the kind of picture-consciousness that we associate with dreaming, whether experienced during the night or as daytime reverie. As difficult as it may sometimes be to control our life of thought, any attempt to control our dream life usually fails. There is no doubt that we are conscious during the dreaming process, because we are often able to remember more or less clearly the dreams which disturb our night's sleep, for memory is undoubtedly part of our conscious experience. Most remarkable, perhaps, is the fact that we create our world of dreams from out of ourselves, and then place ourselves within it as if it were real. We do not doubt the reality of our dreams, for who would deny that the dreams which we all have are just as valid, *in terms of consciousness*, as the world that exists around us when we are awake.

Psychologists and physiologists may debate and argue as they will, again in terms of consciousness, about what the dreaming process is and how it comes about. It is, as always, what we *experience* that counts. And in any case, there is no common agreement among scientists as to how our waking consciousness comes about either. Just how the eye creates pictures of the outside world that so very closely match the material realities of that world has long been, and still is, a great mystery.

The remaining state of consciousness that we experience is of course that of *sleep*. Many people object and say that the sleep state signifies a total lack of consciousness. But if this were entirely true, we would surely have no con sciousness of ever having slept. The key to this problem lies in understanding the significance of memory, and this will be returned to in due course from a spiritual-scientific point of view. The state of sleep may be a thorny scientific problem, but it is a phenomenon with which we are all familiar and is as necessary for sustaining human existence as food and drink.

The astral body is the bearer of our consciousness, and during the time we are awake and active its forces have a *catabolic* effect—that is to say, our daily activities break down countless body cells of various sorts, notably those of the muscles, and we feel fatigued. We know too, of course, that rest and sleep bring about recuperative effects, so that we wake up refreshed and reinvigorated. This is the result of the restorative, 'up-building' function of the etheric body, which has an entirely *anabolic* action. Moreover, during sleep our soul-spiritual members (astral body and ego) to a great extent vacate our corporeal members (etheric and physical bodies), and this is evidenced by the fact that we are not conscious of the outside world while we are asleep.

Animals human and non-human

The term 'non-human animal' is currently very much in fashion, and Darwinism likewise. But in view of the fore-going, it is clear that animals are not, as human beings are, fully independent and responsible for their actions. Humans adapt the environment to their own advantage. Animals adapt themselves to their environment; they are not capable of malice or premeditated criminal acts and are, in every facet of their behaviour, innocent and 'sinless' and not in any way *evil*. Animals, as we have seen, do not possess an ego in any other sense than a 'group-ego', and it is certain that the human capacity for evil is connected with the ego. We are moral beings, and know right from wrong, but morality is unknown in the animal world. Hence we are fully independent and are held responsible for our actions, whereas animals are not.

It cannot be said that animals suffer death as human beings do. When they 'die' they return to the group-ego of the whole species, which is spread throughout the individual creatures that constitute that species. This being so, animals cannot and do not generate karma; they do not have to work out their individual destinies as we do, for it is the whole species which evolves, and this is reflected in the nature, form and behaviour of each member of it. Each individual human being constitutes his or her own 'species' with a unique history stretching back over the ages, undergoing embodiment after embodiment by dint of our being members of the whole human race with its universal character and history.

An important factor connected with the human ego is the faculty of *memory*. Animals have a rudimentary memory of a pictorial nature which they put to practical use, and by which they may learn, but they are seemingly incapable of thinking abstractly. However, we human beings habitually ponder on past experiences and make our plans for future action accordingly, all in full consciousness. We are able to look back over the years and decades, and by means of our powers of memory trace the intricacies of our personal destinies which have led us to where we are today. Our ego, by using the talents of memory, is clearly the agency that maintains the continuity of consciousness throughout our lives, from childhood to old age. As observer and knower as well as initiator of the series of events that goes to make up our personal history, our ego never sleeps, and never dies.

It is worth reiterating the main points concerning the important and essential differences between the animal and human kingdoms. We do this because Darwin's theory of evolution is now widely taught in most schools in a naïve, simplistic fashion, as *fact* rather than *theory*. All Darwin maintained was that human beings and the higher primates have common ancestors, and it is the question of *interpretation* of his evolutionary theory that is at issue rather than any hasty conclusions that have been drawn which suggest that we, as 'naked apes', actually descended from the hairy variety. Darwin provided the facts of the case, but facts are always open to interpretation. And it may rather be a case of turning the whole of current theory on its head, and suggesting that the higher primates have *descended* from us, not we who have *ascended* from them. The notion of a common ancestor would then remain in place and the whole Darwinian theory of evolution be justified—but from a different standpoint.[4]

3.

How Do We Experience Immortality?

> Knowledge of our common life with the dead is one of
> the most important elements which spiritual science has
> to implant into civilization for the future. For those who
> believe that what happens around them occurs only
> through the forces perceived by the senses know
> nothing of reality; they do not know that the dead are
> always at work, always present. They move and have
> their being in a supersensible world. We are not sepa-
> rated from them by our real being, but only by our
> ordinary state of consciousness.[1]

Fear of the unknown

Fear of the known is reputed to be far less than fear of the
unknown, and the fear of death is widespread simply
because of this. Most people wish to hang on to existence as
long as they can, provided it is of reasonable quality, simply
because with death they are facing the unknown. Many
will admit that it is not death itself that they fear; it is rather
the pain and suffering, discomfort and disruption that so
often precedes it. The ultimate fear of death, perhaps, lies in
the supposition that consciousness vanishes at the moment
of expiration, and this is regarded with some trepidation.
However, those people who have experienced what has
come to be known as 'near-death experience' have more or
less the same tale to tell. Most of those who have undergone
this experience speak of deep feelings of bliss, of being

bathed in intense light, of wanting to stay where they are and not 'return' to ordinary life and consciousness.[2]

However, as people get older, anticipation of their own inevitable demise does much to colour their thinking and behaviour. Generally speaking, it is a topic that is not pursued with much enthusiasm, and the taking out of whole-life insurance policies and the making of wills are matters to be faced with varying degrees of disquiet, and emotional and practical problems may also arise. For individuals who are terminally ill, and those members of the family or significant others who care for them or are newly bereaved, there is usually help at hand. Nowadays there are numerous organizations which offer support and advice in the manner of specially trained visiting nurses, hospice accommodation, and suchlike. Much of the work done in these areas has been influenced by the work of Dr Elizabeth Kübler-Ross, who has written and lectured widely on related issues. She identifies five phases which are commonly experienced by those who themselves are facing death as well as those who have 'lost' a loved one, or who undergo the traumas associated with their death.[3] These frequently occur in the order mentioned below, but naturally there are variations and several may happen at the same time. Some moods may be persistent enough to prevent many people from ever coming to terms with their situation, especially if they have no access to counselling.

The first response is often *Denial*, whereby those involved struggle to come to terms with the situation by vainly refusing to admit that it has happened. Closely involved with this stage is *Anger*, perhaps on account of feelings of the unfairness of it all, exasperation and resentment, or helplessness in face of the inevitable, or all of these. Such desperation often gives rise to a tendency to resort to *Bargaining*, an attempt to promise or agree to whatever is required as long as the danger of death is somehow overcome and a degree of wellness restored. As may be imagined, such attitudes as these give rise to *Depression*, a blank hopelessness in realization of the fact that whatever had been hoped for, worked for and wished for will never now come about. Eventually, all the emotional and mental turmoil commonly resolves itself with the recognition that *Acceptance* is the only response to make in face of all the afflictions, ordeals and trials, whatever the consequences. To many people this amounts to gazing into an empty and meaningless blankness, but for others the attaining to an attitude of serene acknowledgement of the situation that allows for the belief or even certainty that death to the material world implies birth in the realms of soul and spirit.

What do we understand by 'death'?

To the ways of thinking of many physiologists death is a matter of 'no working brain, therefore no consciousness and no memory'. Utter extinction of consciousness is expected at the moment of death, and with it no possibility of any further mental or emotional experiences. A very different picture is given by Rudolf Steiner, who investigated death and the life after death very fully and spoke about it often. He reported that, seen from the other side of the threshold of death, the actual passing over is experienced as a moment of great joy and elation, an event later looked back upon with great exhilaration and gladness. So, far from being something to be dreaded, death is something that could inspire very opposite emotions. In his own words:

There is nothing more beautiful in the human being's normal experience of the spiritual world than his perception of death. This victory of spirit over matter, this spiritual light shining up out of the darkness of matter, is the most significant and mightiest thing that can be experienced during the life which the human being passes through between death and a new birth.[4]

Naturally, this kind of experience refers to someone dying of natural causes, and even if death occurs suddenly, 'the separation of these higher members has in fact been prepared for well in advance, so they separate easily and the sense of loss of the physical body is only slight.'

However, the matter is rather different when people who are physically fit and well die suddenly, when death occurs as the result of a tragic accident or, in cases of suicide, by whatever means. An otherwise strong and healthy individual whose whole constitution is well integrated possesses life-forces which are correspondingly powerful, and when the soul and spiritual members are as it were wrenched from their bodily vehicle the experience is bound to be shocking in the extreme. With regard to such circumstances, Steiner had this to say:

But when the separation is sudden and violent as it is with people who have committed suicide, whose whole organism is still healthy and firmly bound together, then immediately after death they feel the loss of the physical body very keenly, and this causes terrible pain. This is a ghastly fate: suicides feel as though they have been plucked out of themselves, and they begin a fearful search for the physical body of which they have been so suddenly deprived.[5]

By implication, people with suicidal tendencies have somehow arrived at the conclusion that their lives have no meaning and purpose, their particular state of mind having arisen from widely diverse personal circumstances. All cases of suicide are fraught with sadness. Everyone has sympathy towards individuals whose existence appears to them as being intolerable, and who seek to escape from their state of hopelessness and despair. Anyone who commits suicide in the belief that they will be taking a leap into oblivion is obliged in the life after death to discover that there is no such way of escape open to them. They will come to the realization that death is a fact only of earthly life, and that the human spirit is indestructible. At the same time they will learn that their hopelessness is not insurmountable, and that their destiny encompasses ways and means of re-covering their confidence in the realities of existence.

The grief and anguish experienced by the mourners may also be tinged with a sense of helplessness, particularly if they had done all they could to impede any apparent sui-cidal propensities. However, they should realize that they can nevertheless be of real help to their loved one who has died in such tragic circumstances. The meditational verse 'In Light of Cosmic Thoughts...' given on page 42 is particularly suitable, as well as that on page 71 commencing 'Upwards to thee strive the love of my soul'. As mentioned elsewhere, the enormous power of love should never be underestimated, for it provides solace and relief as well as soul-spiritual nourishment, of which the dead are especially in great need.

It is a self-evident fact that at the moment of death we are deprived of everything in the way of bodily sensation as well as all power of movement, and this sudden loss is experienced as feelings generated in the soul of intense heat and extreme cold respectively. It is actually the case that the forces borne in the love of those remaining on earth are able to alleviate this very real pain and distress. In the case of those who die from natural causes such feelings of deprivation are usually not so acute. But it goes without saying that everything should be done by those who feel the pangs of bereavement to maintain links with the dead, and these are discussed in the following chapter.

Despite popular belief to the contrary, memories do endure after death. Many people who have, so to say, come back from the dead report similar kinds of conscious experience whereby pictures of incidents in their lives flash through their minds. However, this phenomenon should not be confused with the experience of kamaloka proper. Steiner said: 'Immediately after death the human being is in his etheric body. At this stage, as we know, he looks back and experiences his whole life in a great tableau. Then comes a time during which he only slowly and gradually achieves the consciousness which will be his between death and a new birth.'[6]

Despite all the cleverness of scientists, and all the erudition of scriptural scholars of whatever religion, the phenomena of life and death remain very much a mystery. We all know that every child, gradually formed in its mother's womb and eventually born into the world, must of necessity depart from it. Life inevitably and inexorably implies death: without the experiencing of the one there can be no apprehension of the other. The question arises: if life implies death, can death be said to imply life? Those who read the book of nature aright agree that it does.

We know that we are active during our waking hours because we are conscious of the fact. During our waking hours we are busy with all kinds of activities, and our mental activities engage this waking consciousness. At the same time, what is commonly called our 'unconscious mind' is working ceaselessly and continuously, although we are not aware of this. At night, averred Steiner, we work upon everything that has gone on during the day, and learn even from our unconscious experiences. It can be said with justification that what we call our subconscious is in fact the level of our awareness of our own astral body. Many of the inner promptings and impulses, notions and ideas that rise unbidden into our field of consciousness have their origin in our astral nature. The level of awareness of our etheric body is, however, that of ordinary sleep, when we are unconscious. The level of consciousness *in* our physical body is that of deep sleep, but we may be acutely aware *of* it when pain is experienced through damage or disease.

The kind of consciousness which confirms our awareness of being alive is, it must be said, quite limited. We remember events which occur during our waking lives but are apt to forget that we possess, in addition, a dream-consciousness and a sleep-consciousness. If we didn't, we would never fully appreciate being awake. And with this realization dawns the suspicion that if we have, so to speak, a consciousness that we can explain by reference to our experience of life we may also possess what may be called a death-consciousness. If we recognize in ourselves a certain kind of consciousness that we associate with being alive, why should not the dead also be able to ascribe to themselves a certain kind of consciousness that is associated with being dead? Rudolf Steiner confirmed the ancient maxim that sleep is the small brother of death, which impels us to think that our temporary lack of consciousness during sleep is directly comparable with our permanent loss of waking consciousness at death.[7]

It does not follow that lack of consciousness in the 'lifeless dimension' must be no consciousness at all. As we have seen already, human consciousness on the natural earthly plane of matter exists on three distinct levels, namely, waking, dreaming and sleeping. Any suggestion that other levels do not exist or, if they do, are unattainable is irrational. Steiner averred that there are several more states of consciousness that the human being is capable of attaining, and indicated on many occasions how these may be achieved.

What other states of consciousness?

It may be difficult for us whose spirit and soul are in a very real sense entrapped in our earthly physical body, with all the limitations that it imposes, to imagine other states of consciousness that we are not already familiar with. We are subject to an existence that is bounded by strict parameters in terms of such natural requirements as eating and drinking, sleeping, maintaining an optimal body temperature, maintaining a reasonable state of health and so on. If these requirements are not met, our soul-spiritual principles are not able to maintain their effective hold on our bodily-material vehicle and are compelled to abandon it. The result of this is what we call death, and this simple fact is often made unnecessarily complicated by scientists who persist in trying to define 'brain-death' or whatever in purely materialistic terms.

When a person dies, the corporeal organization, that is to say the physical-material body and its supporting etheric body, is discarded as being no longer tenable, no longer viable in the strictest sense of that word. At this point, perhaps, it is appropriate to mention the tradition of placing bunches and wreaths of flowers and foliage on or near the coffin of a dead person, both before and on the occasion of the funeral. Naturally, it is even more appropriate for the flowers and greenery to be placed inside the coffin, even to the extent of filling it. Elsewhere we mentioned that all members of the plant kingdom possess mineral and etheric bodies only, and our forefathers knew that the etheric forces in all vegetative substance actually assist the dead person's etheric body in leaving the corpse. The reason for this popular custom has long been forgotten, but the tradition has remained—after a fashion, but often one of such an abstract nature as to defeat its original purpose. Recently, the practice has arisen of placing 'floral tributes', or in the case of children teddy-bears and other toys, at the scene of fatal accidents, or perhaps near fences, walls, doorways and so on of the dead person's residence or some other spot that had some association with the individual concerned.

Another popular custom worth mentioning concerns the burning of candles, either as part of a ritual or otherwise, and this extremely widespread tradition takes numerous forms. Such conventions are of course symbolic rather than effectual in character. However, the burning candle possesses a significance of its own in that the candle itself may be taken to represent the solidity and stability of the *body*, the flame itself characterizes the *soul* aglow with the warmth of love, whether wavering or steady, and the light it produces illustrates the human *spirit*—quite literally the light of consciousness which radiates in all directions throughout the universe.

At the moment of death the soul, which roughly equates to the astral or 'consciousness-body', together with the spirit-filled ego which imparts the sense of self, escapes into a realm that is immaterial and supersensory. There the soul expands and eventually reaches the far stretches of the universe, and what was formerly experienced as the outer world becomes its inner world. This 'birth' into the spiritual world stands as a complete reversal of the ordinary birth process, when consciousness is contracted into the limitations of the constraints imposed by the newly acquired physical body.

For the dead, the physical body is rendered redundant immediately, and consciousness of it and apprehension by means of it ceases with the final breath. However, the soul-spiritual principles (astral body and ego) continue to exist; the etheric body also maintains its function as bearer of thoughts and memories. So the dead person remains aware of all that is of a soul and spiritual nature, including certain mental processes upheld by the etheric body.

Now people whom we would normally call 'alive' possess a consciousness (by virtue of their astral body) and a sense of selfhood inherent in their ego. In the case of a so-called 'dead' person, both consciousness and self-awareness are retained. In this way, because both the living and the dead remain in possession of their soul and spiritual principles and therefore share a common area of consciousness, there is no reason why a means of intercommunication should not be established.

Most people do not realize this, of course, and harbour the mistaken belief that the 'dead' may not be contacted except, possibly, by resorting to mediumistic séances and similar practices, which are notoriously unreliable and misleading. It is true that the dead do retain a certain capacity for understanding words expressed in their native language for several years after their death, but this eventually fades and disappears. Then they are only able to 'read' a person's thoughts, and it is noteworthy that the more vividly conceived and strongly held these are the easier they can be grasped.

This fact undermines the claims that mediums make of contacting the dead and passing on their 'messages'. It is far more likely that the medium is being made aware of, and verbalizes, the thoughts and feelings which reside in the depths of the unconscious minds of those present at the particular séance or meeting. Only the perceptions of those individuals who are truly clairvoyant, that is to say capable of investigating the supersensible worlds in full consciousness, can be relied upon. However, as Rudolf Steiner asserted, it is possible for any person, to a limited degree, to 'converse' with those to whom they were closely connected during their earthly lifetime.

Areas of interaction between the living and the dead

Although we are not usually conscious of it, we are in constant communion with those whom we have known while living on the Earth but who are now departed. With regular practice and much patience we may be able to make meaningful contact with them. The initial feeling of closeness with the person who has departed wanes with the passage of time, as other interests claim the bereft person's attention. This is perfectly natural in a way, because the world of physical reality is immediate and familiar, inviting as well as demanding, and therefore all the more heeded, until eventually only memories of the departed remain. On the other hand, it is much easier for those who have died to remain in contact, not only with the living but with other disembodied souls with whom they have shared a common destiny. If significant connections existed during their earthly lives, their closeness allows for a kind of inter-mingling of souls after death, a kind of soul-spiritual sharing at will.

It is in similar fashion that departed souls are able to partake of the soul-spiritual life of those whom they left behind on Earth. It is really so that they are able to think another's thoughts, especially if they concern matters and things which are of a spiritual nature. Steiner laid great emphasis on the fact that normally only those souls—embodied and disembodied—who have previously had connections while in an earthly environment are capable of the kind of intermingling mentioned just now. It is impossible for disembodied souls who were not connected by destiny during their earthly life to hold any kind of interactive relationship. This is logical enough, because meaningful human relationships spring only from our soul-spiritual natures, our ego in particular. The dead are able only to reach downwards to the level of thoughts and feelings of those remaining on Earth, that is to say, to the astral level.

It goes without saying that, as they have no access to what is material, the dead cannot apprehend thoughts that involve financial transactions, moving house, buying clothes and suchlike. Everything of a vegetative nature is also denied to them, for any entity which does not possess a 'soul-nature' in the manner of an astral organization remains inaccessible to their consciousness. The following meditational verse by Rudolf Steiner sums up much of what has been discussed:

> In Light of Cosmic Thoughts
> Now weaves the soul
> That was united with me upon Earth.

May the warm life of my heart
Stream outward to thy soul;
To warm thy cold,
And mitigate thy heat.
In spiritual worlds
May my thoughts live in thine,
And thy thoughts live in mine.[8]

The dead and the world of the Angels

The consciousness of the so-called dead is able to extend much further upwards, so to speak, than downwards. After entering the supersensible realms departed souls are able progressively to intermingle and interact with the so-called Hosts of Heaven, members of the hierarchies of exalted spiritual beings which stand above our own. Their nine rankings are as follows:

	Biblical Term	*Spiritual-scientific Term*
First	Seraphim	Spirits of Love
Hierarchy	Cherubim	Spirits of Harmony
	Thrones	Spirits of Will
Second	Dominions	Spirits of Wisdom
Hierarchy	Powers or Mights	Spirits of Motion
	Authorities	Spirits of Form
Third	Principalities	Spirits of Personality
Hierarchy		(Time Spirits)
	Archangels	Spirits of Fire
		(Folk Spirits/Souls)
	Angels	Spirits of Life
		(or Twilight)

Rudolf Steiner often referred to human beings as the Hierarchy of Love and Freedom, for these two enormously complex factors figure large in our personal and social lives, as even a moment's reflection will show. He asserted that not only can departed souls be supported by us in a more or less conscious manner, but they also feel greatly sustained by spiritual beings belonging to the Third Hierarchy, namely, the Angels, Archangels and Archai (Principalities).[9] The traditional belief that every individual has a Guardian Angel, who acts as a guide during earthly life as well as through the worlds of soul and spirit after death, was confirmed by Steiner from his own researches. He also identified the remaining hierarchies, giving them names in accordance with their main function or characteristic.

Steiner observed that in his time people found it very difficult to acquire knowledge of the spiritual worlds, and this appears still to be the case, in spite of the vast treasury of knowledge which he made available to the world. We may not be able to experience the spiritual worlds at first hand, but at least we can study and reflect on what he was able to tell us concerning his own investigations into those supersensory realms.

He was tireless in his encouragement of those who wished to follow a path of spiritual development, and maintained that only to realize the certainty of the Eternal in one's own being was already of great value. It now seems that interest in spiritual science is being rekindled as more individuals are confirming aspects of its findings from personal experience. For those who remain content to read and hear about the spiritual worlds rather than attempt their own investigations, the following verse from Rudolf Steiner, 'At the Ringing of Bells', expresses something of the devotion to highest nobility in terms of ethics and morality that must accompany the spiritual researcher:

> To wonder at beauty,
> To stand guard over truth,
> To look up to the noble,
> To decide for the good:
> Leads us on our journey
> To goals for our life,
> To right in our doing,
> To peace in our feeling,
> To light in our thinking;
> And teaches us trust
> In the guidance of God
> In all that there is
> In the wide World-All,
> In the soul's deep soil.[10]

Laws physical and metaphysical

In the earthly world we are subject to natural laws, e.g. the law of gravity, and we trust in their reliability and, for the most part, predictability. Modern science has contributed enormously to the elaboration of the so-called laws of nature, and its discoveries deserve our gratitude and admiration. Now Rudolf Steiner was emphatic that order is a principal characteristic of the spiritual world, and this should come as no surprise. Just as the expression 'law and order' is universally recognized as characteristic of the material world, so it can with equal validity be applied to spiritual realms. The fact that nature encompasses both material and spiritual worlds, both seen and unseen, is easily overlooked: ultimately, there is no meaning to such words as *supernatural*, *supernormal* and *paranormal*. The law of cause and effect, for example, is operational in the spiritual world also; the ancient maxim 'As above, so below' holds good throughout the whole of Creation.

One of the most important tenets of spiritual science is this: at all times and in all circumstances, spirit is antecedent to matter. This fact is not usually noticed for the simple reason that the solidity and clarity of material facts captures our attention first. Spiritual experiences, being of a delicate nature, often pass unnoticed. The law of cause and effect as it manifests in the invisible worlds of the spirit is not easy for us to discern, but it does exist. A well-known example of its working is the law of karma, or self-created destiny. When considered together with its twin concept of reincarnation it makes very good sense in terms of fairness and justice.

The significance of moral and religious values in the life after death

At a certain stage in the progression of departed souls through the spiritual realms, whether or not individuals have been actively concerned with moral questions during their life on earth becomes of substantial importance. This means that people who have embraced values which may loosely be referred to as *religious*, whether or not they were associated with any organized group, find themselves in a happier position after death than those who did not. Rudolf Steiner often pointed out that those who had been materialists and, by implication, hedonists who had, for example, made a kind of religion of sport, entertainment, the pursuit of pleasure and the like, find themselves lonely and isolated, and obliged to live a solitary existence in the heavenly worlds.[11]

On the other hand, the common feature of religious movements and organizations of whatever confession or creed, or in whatever part of the world, is fellowship. People come together to worship, honour or venerate the deity they choose, and thereby form congregations or gatherings to experience the companionship which arises from a shared religious or ideological outlook. This common bond is genuinely re-experienced at a certain stage on the journey between death and rebirth, where various communities are formed out of a particular sense of belonging and mutual understanding, repeating in a very real sense their affiliations enjoyed during their earlier earthly lives (see Chapter 5).

This particular period of comradely association is followed by another, in which certain experiences are open to us if we have made only a fragile connection with the Being known as Christ. What Steiner often called the 'Christ Event' was that which featured the Incarnation, Crucifixion and Resurrection of an exalted Spiritual Being who united His destiny with that of the Earth itself. This Event did of course form the basis of an organized religion which, as he indicated, is unique in that it finds its roots in the whole history of the universe. However, this can be no cause for feelings of superiority among Christians, for he also stressed that the Christian religion is still, even after two thousand years, at a positively embryonic stage in its development.

Steiner approached the whole enigma surrounding Christ's Incarnation and subsequent related events purely and solely from his standpoint as supersensible researcher, and not from any kind of scriptural, historical or other sort of doctrinal basis. That is to say, he regarded the mission of Christ as having, in essence and substance, nothing whatever to do with religious *belief*, past or present, but that it is of cosmic significance, and constituted a particularly important occurrence in terms of the development of humanity as a whole, and indeed of our very planet.

In brief, his research showed that the Being that came to be called the Christ, the long-awaited Messiah, was none other than the Sun Being (the Light of the World) that had been worshipped in previous ages in the Mystery Centres of the Persians, Egyptians and Greeks, and in more recent times the Teutonic, Norse, Celtic and other pagan cultures previous to His descent to Earth. At the Baptism by John in the River Jordan, the Christ Being achieved His incarnation into the body of Jesus of Nazareth, therein to dwell until His crucifixion. Since the Resurrection He has remained on our planet, present in the etheric realms but unseen to all but those with supersensible perception. ('Lo, I am with you always, even unto the end of the age,' Matt. 28:20.) Christ, the Being of Light and Love, was fully aware of the purposes of His mission, as indicated in the Gospel of John 8:14: 'For I know whence I come and whither I go...'

Anyone who strives while on Earth towards a full understanding and appreciation of the deeds of Christ, whether in religious terms or those of comprehension, will so to speak qualify to experience His presence between death and rebirth. They will be capable of sustaining consciousness throughout their passage through the supersensible worlds after death.[12] They will come to understand the real meaning of fellowship based on mutual love and regard, on free acts of giving which place the needs of others before their own.

Can we actually experience immortality?

Now death has meaning only on the earthly plane. As spiritual beings we cannot be destroyed or otherwise annihilated, but what we may be subject to after passing into the spiritual worlds is a *diminution of consciousness*. In Rudolf Steiner's own words:

> Many today speak of immortality when they can merely admit that the being of the human soul passes through the gate of death and then finds some place or other in the universal All. But every creature does that. That which is united with the crystal is dissolved; the plant that fades passes into the universe; the animal at death passes over into the universe. For mankind it is different. Immortality has a meaning for human beings only if they can carry their consciousness through the gate of death. Think of an immortal human soul that was unconscious after death; such immortality would have absolutely no meaning.[13]

In view of what has been discussed, we have the clue as to just what it is that enables those who have died to maintain their consciousness while in the spiritual worlds, and that can be expressed in a single word: *love*. In the first phase after death a meaningful relationship with others in terms of social interaction involving fellowship is sufficient to maintain a degree of consciousness. In the second we need to have established a significant measure of association with Christ, whether within or without the religious life.

The common element or factor is that of love in some form or other, but always within a social context. The verb 'to love' is transitive, which implies some kind of carrying over of the action of its meaning. In other words, it is impossible to love in the abstract—we must love *someone* or *something*. To give oneself up to self-love has the consequence in the supersensory realms that one is conscious *only* of one's own existence—hence the feelings of loneliness and isolation.

Scriptures of all religions stress that God loves us all. All members of humanity are His children, and are exhorted to love God with heart, soul and mind (Matt. 22:37, Mark 12:30), and to love our neighbours as ourselves (Mark 12:33). The very feelings and deeds of love towards God and our neighbours accentuate our sense of selfhood and individuality. Love must be expressed in altruistic deeds, otherwise it will be tainted by elements of self-love and self-interest. As we carry our love of God through death, so we carry with us that which kindles love within—our individuality.

By cultivating spiritual values and by deeds of unconditional love and devotion in the interests of others while on earth, our individuality acquires the power to sustain consciousness during the life between death and birth. It is too late to attempt to achieve this while on the spiritual plane, irrespective of the fact that the soul of the departed is surrounded by spiritual beings of all kinds. Academic knowledge alone, even spiritual knowledge, is not sufficient for this if love and deeds of love are not forthcoming.

It is worth calling to mind that in the times prior to the advent of Christ on the Earth, souls who had passed through the gate of death felt completely isolated and enveloped in darkness. This condition was known to the Greeks and the Hebrews as Hades and Sheol respectively, and regarded by all as the Land of the Shades. During the Christian era the sense of self or individuality was becoming more and more intense, and egotism would have become rampant, increasing in strength with every new incarnation, had not the mission of Christ directed humanity in the opposite direction—towards universal brotherhood. In this way, through His message of love, he brought the light of consciousness and the balanced warmth of fellowship into the Land of the Shades. It is therefore easy to see why Christ is worthy of the epithet 'Light of the World'. His deed on the earth brought the hope of true immortality to all people by making possible the *continuity of consciousness* to souls passing through death and onwards to a new birth. All these notions were gathered up by Rudolf Steiner into beautiful form in the following meditation:

> I gaze upon thee in the spiritual world
> In which you are.
> May my love allay your warmth,
> May my love allay your coldness.
> May it reach out to you, and help you
> To find your way
> Through Spirit-darkness
> To Spirit-light.[14]

4.

Achieving Communion with Those Who Have Died

> May love of hearts reach out to love of souls,
> May warmth of love ray out to Spirit light.
> Even so would we draw near to you,
> Thinking with you Thoughts of Spirit,
> Feeling in you the Love of Worlds,
> Consciously at one with you
> Willing in silent Being.[1]

The dead really are with us

Naturally it is not easy for us to transfer our consciousness into the spiritual realms in which the dead carry on with their own style of existence, but the effort should none-theless be made. To those left behind on Earth, notwith-standing the pain and grief they feel inwardly because of it, the departure of loved ones is a purely external event. Those who have passed through the gate of death have, in a single instant, found themselves bereft of their physical body with all sensations associated with it, including pain and suffering. To them it is decidedly an inner event, a soul-event.

Just as the spiritual world 'dies' to us when we are born into physical life on Earth, so when we die in the Earthly sense we are born into, or rather 'give birth to', a world of soul and spirit within ourselves. What was our inner world now becomes our outer world, and vice versa. While on earth we experience the world outside and all around us; after death we perceive the world as being within us. The whole process becomes easier to understand when we consider that the needs of a newborn baby are all met from the world outside it, whereas a mature person has, by reason of their experiences during their lifetime, developed their own private, microcosmic inner world within the greater, public world. It is this inner world, which is obviously of that person's own creation, which becomes as it were their environment after death.

Rudolf Steiner observed that many people have no real apprehension of the fact that when souls pass over into the spiritual realms they find there other souls, many of whom they recognize. Not to appreciate this situation, he asserted, is like contending that new-born babies likewise find no one on the earth to receive them there. After death we have around us a world of pure being, of pure soul, and the loss of our previous material environment is keenly felt. Naturally, the astonishment is greatest for those who denied the spirit while here in physical life, for they find themselves in a world which they had denied, and which, therefore, is completely unknown to them.[2]

Here we find another example of the principle of reversal or oppositeness which we frequently encounter where spiritual laws and concerns are seen to differ from physical-material ones. When we depart the spiritual realms and are born into the earthly environment, we already possess senses and sense-organs which are all ready for us to use and develop. Conversely, when we are 'born' into the spiritual worlds at death we are entirely dependent on the degree and extent of spiritual development we have attained to on Earth for our ability to 'find our way around'. Individuals who have been convinced materialists during their Earthly life find themselves, on arrival in a purely spiritual environment, in virtual darkness. During their earthly lives they have not become acquainted with spiritual ideas, and are therefore so to speak 'sightless' in the soul-spiritual environment they encounter after death.

Steiner was careful to point out the importance of realizing the differences existing between the death of an adult and that of a child. In the case of adults, and older people in particular, the very fact that they are strongly drawn to the spiritual worlds empower them more easily to approach us who are left. Of course we 'miss' them, but the pain is ours, albeit an egotistical pain. In the case of children it is *we* who feel always close to them. Children who have died have had little experience of the world to which they were drawn so strongly before birth, and have formed only very limited connections with individuals other than the immediate family and household. They remain near us and linger in our earthly environment because of these affinities before returning to the spiritual world, and so in a spiritual sense are not lost to their dear ones.

Children have had neither time nor opportunity to develop what might be expressed as truly meaningful relationships. They have not incarnated very deeply, and lack understanding of the material world and its inhabitants, of which they have had only very limited experience. The departed souls of the children feel pain on account of their deprivation and this communicates itself to the parents, who naturally also feel pain. By reason of the fact that children have lived, and are still living, in close association—almost to the point of identification—with those whom they loved and still love, they themselves feel the pain and sorrow of the parents and significant others and are thereby comforted and consoled.

As it would be impossible to say much about the career and achievements of children who have died, a memorial service that concentrates on individual achievements would scarcely seem appropriate. Steiner considered it more fitting, in this case, to hold a service that is ritualistic in character, for the gestures and general spiritual atmosphere pervading such a service would be more meaningful for the departed souls of children.[3] There inevitably remains the matter of further reincarnation, and it is often the case that individuals who have died very young seek early re-embodiment and, if the opportunity arises, may well be reborn into the same family or that of close relatives or friends.

Older people, longing as they were for the spiritual worlds, move further away from the earthly, but they are also able to maintain their bonds with those they have left behind, which are likely to be stronger in any case. Furthermore, their powers of perception are more powerful than those of infants or young children, who have only recently left their spiritual home and have experienced comparatively little of their material environment during their brief earthly sojourn. Individuals who attain to a reasonably healthy old age undergo a gradual disincarnation process, and by reason of this they feel an increasingly greater affinity with spiritual rather than material concerns. They are of course acutely conscious of their impending demise, and may be able to prepare themselves emotionally and mentally for this. They may be able to talk about death quite freely, frequently in a mood of quiet anticipation that they will be welcomed by loved ones who have already departed—much as a newborn baby is normally welcomed by loving parents who were born a generation previously.

As mentioned earlier, mature individuals do not lose us

when they die. They are all around us, and indeed enter into our very souls and are able to commune with us even though we may not be aware of it. In such circumstances a traditional memorial service is entirely appropriate, and often on such an occasion the presence of the departed soul is strongly felt by those present. Rituals and liturgies by themselves tend to be of a general nature and universal in character, and for this reason it is good that biographical aspects be brought to the consciousness of those present in as vivid a way as possible. If the dead person left specific instructions as to what they wished to be done, then these should receive careful consideration.

Although strong sentiments and feelings are aroused when a mature person dies, those of grief and sorrow, anguish and heartache should be tempered by the realization that destiny has brought the situation about, and this should be fully taken into account. Very often it is a case of 'happy release' from extreme pain and suffering on the part of the dead person, in which case the sense of loss is to some extent mitigated. There is, understandably enough, an element of self-pity contained in our grief, but with the passage of time this also gradually diminishes. Paramount in our thoughts and feelings should be the knowledge that death in the material world implies birth in the spiritual world, and that it is only the selfish side of us which resents our being inconvenienced by their passing. We should not 'wish them back', for such feelings are communicated to the dead person and serve only to retard their progress.

Can we establish connections with those who have died?

Generally speaking, it is easier for those who have died to approach us than it is for us to draw near to them. In the majority of cases the reason for their passing over into the supersensory worlds of the spirit is because they felt overwhelmingly drawn in that direction. At the same time, however, they retain certain affinities with the material world they have recently left. It is invariably the case, whether we die old or young, that there is a residue of important or significant unexercised thoughts, perceptions and feelings which were left unrealized. If these are not to be lost, but rather brought forward to some degree of maturity by those remaining on earth who have karmic ties with the originator of such thoughts and feelings, endeavours can nevertheless be made to establish connections and means of communication in a quite conscious manner, and Rudolf Steiner gave definite indications as to how this may be achieved.[4]

Those who have gone through the gate of death find themselves in a state of ceaseless activity.[5] They are obliged to be continually creative in order to construct their own world, their own environment, which is entirely of a soul or spiritual nature—that is to say, of pure being. Here on earth we have no difficulty in perceiving our environment, thanks to our efficient and reliable sense organs. True to the principle of reversal, if we wish to perceive beings and events in the spiritual world we find it very difficult, if not impossible. We have to practise meditational and other exercises with unflagging patience if we are to become consciously aware in the supersensory world. However, those loved ones and friends who have died, already accomplished at perceiving that which is of a spiritual nature, have little difficulty in apprehending us here on the physical plane—but such perception is necessarily confined to our soul and spirit. Our etheric and physical bodies inevitably remain beyond their range and scope.

It is the embodied friends who find that they have to make a considerable effort to establish any meaningful connection. It is comparatively easy for the departed souls to apprehend loving thoughts and memories of those still on Earth with whom they were in some significant fashion related, and this gives them great satisfaction. This is why it is good to bring our departed loved ones to mind clearly and often, to visit places which both parties enjoyed going to, and to talk about incidents they shared with other friends who were present and able to recall them. For those who earnestly wish to establish some kind of link with their dear ones who have departed, it is even better if they actively practise the exercises and some of the meditations and verses which Rudolf Steiner himself devised for such use and which we have taken care to include in this book.

Within this context, it is worth quoting him:

> Each time dead people contact a remembrance of themselves in the souls of those to whom they were in some way connected on Earth, it is always as if something streams over to them which beautifies their life, enhancing its value. And as to us here, beauty comes from Art, so to the dead, beauty streams to them from that which rays forth out of the hearts and souls of those who keep them in memory . . . It is therefore important for the dead to find their image in those souls who still remain here.[6]

We and the dead need one another

Those who have crossed the threshold of death actually need and long for the love and the thoughts of those who were close to them on Earth. Although they find themselves surrounded by the light of the spirit, they need also what the living can give them. Materialistic thoughts have no reality for them, and so do not reach them. However, loving thoughts of a spiritual nature are like food for them, without which they feel deprived even to the point of hunger, of craving for spiritual sustenance.

When we go to sleep at night, the ideas and thoughts which have passed through our consciousness in our waking hours begin to live, to be vital, independent entities. Then the souls of the dead draw near and share in these ideas, feeling nourished as they perceive them. If we have occupied ourselves with spiritual thoughts and ideas, those who have died, and especially those who were close to us, are nurtured and sustained by them. The wholesome habit of practising evening or bedtime prayer, far from being out of date, is of great benefit for both the living and the dead.

However, this relationship is by no means one-sided, for those who have died can in turn be of very real help to the living. Rudolf Steiner averred that the dead frequently turn their spiritual gaze towards those still living on the earth. He urged that we always bear this in mind, and cultivate feelings of responsibility for all that we do in relationship to the dead, particularly in our efforts to establish communication with them. The benefits are mutual, in that we who are living receive life-giving power, and the dead benefit from the effects of our own spiritual strivings.[7]

It is also of common benefit if bereaved individuals actually read to those who have died. Obviously, the subject-matter should be of a spiritually uplifting or inspirational nature, and appropriate for reader and the ones being read to. Rudolf Steiner encouraged anthroposophists to read spiritual science to their departed relatives and friends, even if they did not embrace such ideas while on earth. The dead feel the need of spiritual sustenance, and are particularly attentive if the overall mood is one of warm feeling.

Such reading, which can take place at any time, need not be an actual reading aloud, provided that the thoughts in the mind of the reader are sharp and clear. Words in their native language are comprehended particularly well for a few years after death. But it is most important for readers to maintain a strong sense of presence of those they are reading to, even down to actual visualization. What really matters is thinking thoughts through to the end; to skim through them is not good enough.[8] The subject-matter must be worked through word by word, even if not actually articulated. Silent reading can be effective if we formulate clear-cut concepts, for thereby the dead are enabled to follow us thought by thought.

From time to time ideas may occur to us more or less spontaneously which we attribute to ourselves, whereas they may well have been planted in our souls by a close relative or friend who has died. As so often when we are dealing with the invisible, intangible, supersensory worlds, what arises on the earthly plane is experienced as a *reversal* of what, with our materially based thinking, we would normally assume to be the case. Rudolf Steiner's own words are clear on this:

In the physical world, when we speak to a human being from physical body to physical body, we know that the words come from ourselves; when the other person speaks to us, we know that the words come from him. The whole relationship is reversed when we are speaking with one who has died. The expression 'when we are speaking' can truthfully be used, but the relationship is reversed. When we put a question to, or say something to a 'dead' person, what we say comes from him, comes to us from him. He inspires into our soul what we ask him, what we say to him. And when he answers us or says something to us, this comes out of our own soul. It is a process with which a human being in the physical world is quite unfamiliar. In order to establish communication with those who have died, we must adapt ourselves to hear from them what we ourselves say, and to receive from our own soul what they answer.[9]

It is this seemingly strange and unconventional procedure which supplies the reason as to why the establishment of links of communication with departed souls is so seldom recognized. The 'dead' are always there and available to us—among us, around us, and indeed within us, wherever we are and whatever the time of day. But the curious reversal of patterns we take for granted in ordinary life invariably gives rise to difficulties and misconceptions, and considerable perseverance is called for if conscious communication is to be achieved. In practice, of course, it is our love for those who have crossed the threshold which motivates us, and the ensuing blessings will be mutual. The following meditation by Rudolf Steiner indicates how desirable it is for us to establish connections between those of us, embodied and disembodied alike, who have had significant relationships with one another:

> Into the fields of Spirit will I send
> The faithful love we found on Earth,
> Uniting soul with soul.
> And you will find my loving thought
> When from the Spirit-lands of light
> You hither turn your seeking soul
> To find that which you seek in me.[10]

The practice of meditation brings many benefits

Rudolf Steiner deplored the fact that few people are aware of the possibilities of establishing links with the dead, going so far as to declare that Earthly life in general is actually impoverished if contacts with the dead are not sought and maintained. Many people who grasp the implications of this feel that they should do what they can to establish communion with those dear to them who have died, regarding this as a loving duty. The whole issue is of course highly personal, so it is up to individuals to organize their activities as it best suits them. Taking the measures needed for establishing connection with the dead is an inspiring activity as well as being of enormous benefit to all concerned. Steiner's words regarding this are very encouraging: 'When, by means of meditation, individuals rise to be united with the spirit, they bring to life the eternal within themselves, which is limited by neither birth nor death.'[11]

We do well to remind ourselves that those who have departed have relatively easy access to our soul-spiritual nature, whereas we who remain have to make sustained efforts to reach them by means of concentration, contemplation and meditation. However, there is no need to feel daunted by what may well be a new experience. All that is needed falls readily under the heading of love for those with whom we would seek to establish what in effect is a new kind of relationship. During life we have been very close to them, and have worked for one another's benefit. Now arises the opportunity to continue this work, and give ourselves over gladly to carrying it out.

An attitude of thankfulness for all with which we were—and indeed still are—favoured can be strongly influenced by recalling fond memories. Gradually a mood of devotion, love for the task, and the wish to forge new links will prevail as an inexhaustible source of encouragement, hope and resolve. We need to bear in mind that once we have decided to make the effort to develop a relationship with the dead, we should try to remain faithful to our commitments. Establishing such a connection is a noble and desirable act in every way, but it demands perseverance and the ability to wait for results with patience and tranquillity.

Subjects for meditative reflection are to be found in plenty in religious scriptures and the writings of saints and mystics. Rudolf Steiner himself left a splendid treasury of material eminently suitable for both spiritual enrichment and as an aid for developing spiritual insights. There is also an abundance of sound advice and reliable guidance available in his books, to help us with the practice of meditation and the development of our powers of concentration needed for this.[12] It bears repetition that only thoughts with spiritual content are capable of being used in establishing a common ground between the dead and the living, which functions as a kind of meeting-place.

When we adopt a regular pattern of meditation, it is a good idea to establish a certain routine. It is always of great importance to create the right mood, both emotional and mental. We should seat ourselves, preferably on an upright chair, and make sure that there is little likelihood of being disturbed by the hustle and bustle of daily life. Those racing thoughts, and any cares or anxieties, should be pushed away, and a mood of peace and quiet allowed to form. Only then can we concentrate earnestly and fully on our chosen theme for meditation. Any images that are formed should be sharp and vivid, and thoughts need to be clear and well-defined. Resist the tendency to wander from the central issue, and when the session is felt to have come to a natural stop, take definite steps to disengage from the whole process. If strong feelings have been experienced, it is good to remain quiet and allow them to vibrate in the soul until they die away.

By practising meditation at certain times of the day in regular fashion, these moments are built into the rhythms of our etheric and astral bodies. The result is that, far from regarding our meditation as a daily chore, we come to look forward to it. By patient application, a genuine link between the dead and the living can be established, and communication achieved. However, we must be careful, in our eagerness to make connections, not to allow expectation to lead us into merely imagining that we are receiving 'messages'. The gifts of the spirit are bestowed on us in unexpected or even surprising ways, so it is a matter of working, watching, and waiting.

Rudolf Steiner often spoke about the spiritual worlds 'approaching us', which may seem to be a strange expression to employ. But it is no mere metaphor, for this is literally the case. When we are conscious of the spiritual world, during certain periods after death or while exercising spiritual perception, it is not we who 'move'. We attract things and beings of a spiritual nature towards us by means of our thinking activity, and they do actually approach us; we remain as it were quite immobile.

What Steiner called 'restfulness of soul' is an important ingredient for success in spiritual exercises. The quieter, calmer and more inwardly and outwardly serene we are, the better. Here is a meditation he gave in the interests of maintaining the required mood:

I carry Rest within me;
I bear within myself
Forces which give me strength.
Myself will I fill
With the warmth of these forces;
Myself will I permeate
With the power of my will.
And I will feel
How Rest outpours itself
Throughout my being,
If I strengthen myself
To come upon Rest
As a force within me,
Through the power of my striving.[13]

This meditation can also be used as a counterbalance to the stress of modern life, which has brought about such conditions as 'sensory overload' and 'information fatigue', which do so much to undermine our general health and well-being.

The backward review

Of the highest possible importance is the regular practice usually referred to as the 'backward review' or 'retrospect', an exercise which should take no more than ten minutes. It is carried out immediately before sleep, and entails re-experiencing the events of the day in pictures or images as vividly as possible *in reverse order,* from that moment until waking up the same morning. Just as sleep may be regarded as the small brother of death, such a backward review may reasonably be regarded as a kind of 'mini-kamaloka' (kamaloka is described in Chapter 5), for it should function as a 'sensitizer' to errors in our behaviour and render us more sympathetic, or better still empathetic, towards those with whom we have dealings during the day. This exercise will also help us to become familiar with the 'reversal' factor invariably involved when the actual spiritual worlds themselves are encountered. The main thing to remember is that the most significant events of the day should pass before the inner observant eye in as much detail as possible, while disregarding trivial or minor happenings. Every effort should be made to observe ourselves as if by a third party and from above, and to ensure that no event of real significance is overlooked.

All this may sound relatively effortless, but in practice it is all too easy for our mind to wander from the strict pattern of events as they occurred, or we may even fall asleep! If we persist, however, our powers of concentration and our ability to form mental images will improve considerably.

Moments of particular significance

Rudolf Steiner often drew attention to two very important moments for conversing with the dead, especially when it involves receiving communications from them. These are the brief seconds that lie between sleeping and waking, and the reverse, between waking and sleeping. For the most part we do not notice them, as we slip so easily into forgetfulness immediately before going to sleep; and on waking we all too often find our senses being bombarded by sense-perceptions which tend to obliterate anything in the way of messages from those who have departed. It is possible, however, to develop a delicate sensitivity during these fleeting moments that occur immediately before waking and just before falling asleep.

It is more common to be especially perceptive—and receptive—at the instant of waking. If everything around is

quiet and dark, this subtle and elusive moment of awareness
is more easily captured by our consciousness. It is important
in any case to know that at this time all kinds of 'message'
may be communicated, whether from a loved one who has
died, a close friend or relation, or even one's Guardian
Angel. Such impressions should be remembered and given
careful consideration and attempts be made to put them into
a context that is meaningful. It is well known, of course, that
'inspirations' may occur at any time during the night, and
many people set much store by these. However, in the rush
to write such 'revelations' down—for they are all too easily
and quickly forgotten—they may slip the mind and be gone.

When we mean to convey some kind of message or
question to a dead person, our thoughts and ideas need to be
permeated through and through with feeling, and that
feeling is invariably *love*. Whatever we wish to convey must
be imbued not only with heartfelt earnestness but also with
will, resolution and inner conviction. We must consciously
and energetically *send* our message, and imbue it with as great
a degree of feeling as we are capable.[14] Its content is best
directed towards that in which there is a common interest,
and not anything abstract, trivial, or to do with everyday
practical affairs. Visualizations of actual occasions of toge-
therness should energetically be brought to mind. This may
be done at any time of the day, but the message or question
should preferably be well thought out and formulated in
advance for it will remain as it were pending until the very
moment of falling asleep, when it will be passed on.

The matter of dreams involving those who have died are
invariably of interest, though it must be said that this particular area is fraught with misconception. Very often
people imagine that a particular dream is meant to convey
some kind of message from the dead person to them, when

it is more likely that they themselves have originated it. The whole subject is difficult and complex, for dreaming occurs below our usual level of conscious awareness and therefore beyond our control.

A very special exercise

The following exercise given by Rudolf Steiner for those suffering bereavement provides a good example of the frame of mind we must adopt if we are to communicate effectively with the dead. The prevailing mood needs to be one of great earnestness and strength of feeling. These are his actual words:

> Let yourself go quiet three times a day, the last time just before dropping off to sleep, so that you take these thoughts with you into the world of the spirit. The best thing is to go to sleep with this in mind:

> *My love, given in sacrifice,*
> *Shall be woven into the forms*
> *That now envelop you,*
> *Cooling all warmth,*
> *Warming all coldness.*
> *Live supported by love,*
> *Given the gift of light,*
> *As you ascend.*

It is important to have the right kind of feeling when you think or say the words 'warmth' and 'coldness'. They do not mean physical warmth and coldness, but something like the warmth and coldness we know and experience in our feelings, bearing in mind that it is difficult for someone who is in a physical body to have a real idea of what these qualities mean to someone who is no longer inhabiting his or her body. Those who have left their body must first of all realize that the astral or soul element which still remains with them continues to be active, in spite of the fact that it no longer possesses its physical, bodily instruments in the form of limbs and other material agencies. Many things we seek to achieve here on earth are accomplished with the aid of these physical instruments. After death they have gone. Not to have physical sense organs is like—but we can only say *like*—a feeling of parching thirst in the soul. Those are the powerful sensations of heat experienced once we are disembodied. In the same way our will, formerly used to having physical members at its disposal which allow us to achieve these ends, then no longer has those purely bodily components. These feelings of deprivation produce a sensation of coldness in the soul.

It is specifically with regard to these sensations that the living are able to help. These feelings are not merely the outcome of a particular life; they are connected with the mysteries of the incarnation. And because of this it is possible to help those who have left their body...[15]

Thus, as we give support by virtue of our love in the ways mentioned in the passage above, we may be sure that this support is reciprocated; and indeed many people feel this. The reference to light refers to spiritual light, or the capacity for those who have died to be aware of, to be actually conscious of, the spiritual worlds in which they are now living. Those who during their Earthly existence rejected religious ideas or spirituality in general find themselves surrounded by dimness and even darkness, and feel lonely and fearful in consequence. Departed souls who are already familiar with issues appertaining to the spirit are empowered more ably to 'ascend' smoothly and serenely through the various 'regions' of the soul and spiritual worlds towards eventual reincarnation.[16]

Notice that Rudolf Steiner mentions love on two occasions in the verse above, and with very good reason. He described love as being 'a child of the spirit', and even a moment's reflection will confirm that this quality, more than any other, represents the loftiest and most significant emotion that we human beings possess. It should come as no surprise, therefore, that our main link with those whose spirit has left their body is by means of and through love. Steiner laid stress on this fact, and often spoke of the enormous power of love quite concretely, describing how this noble and lofty feeling may be harnessed to the benefit of those who have passed through the Gate of Death. Needless to say, love should be universal, unrestricted and freely given; and it is this sacrificial kind of love which we offer to our loved ones who have departed. 'From deeds of love we have nothing to benefit our own egotism, yet the world has all the more from them. Spiritual research tells us that love is for the whole world what the sun is for external life. No soul could any longer grow and flourish anywhere if love were taken from the world. Love is the moral sun of the universe.'[17] Here is a supplemental verse:

> Upward to thee strive the love of my soul,
> Upward to thee flow the stream of my love!
> May they sustain thee,
> May they uphold thee
> In heights of hope,
> In spheres of love.[18]

In many respects the fundamental theme of Love is complemented by that of Light, not only in the sense of enlightenment of our consciousness in respect of earthly and spiritual concerns, but also of the capacity of those who have died to be conscious of the spirit world in which they are now living. In both cases there is the connecting quality of *purity*. The exercising of a love that is pure, that is to say untainted by egotism, always enhances the light of consciousness, and the raising of our level of conscious awareness unfailingly brings a greater appreciation of the power of love in the world. It is because of this that the theme of purity was frequently taken up by Rudolf Steiner in many helpful and illuminating meditations. Here is an example:

Evening

Within the Godhead of the World,
There shall I find Myself
Wherein I rest.
The godhood of my soul outpours
In purest Love to all that is.
Shimmers the Godhead of the World
In purest Light outpoured.

Morning

In purest outpoured Light
Shimmers the Godhead of the World.
In purest Love to all that is
Outpours the godhood of my soul.
I rest within the Godhead of the World.
There shall I find Myself
Within the Godhead of the World.[19]

Here it can be seen that our sense of identity is quite separate from the Divinity, for in the Godhead I *rest*, I *find* myself. This accentuates the fact that we are able to preserve our sense of individuality after death, and are not merely assimilated (as is sometimes thought to be the case) into the universal All. The particular significance of establishing contact with the Divinity through the Being of Christ while we are still on the earth, as discussed in the previous chapter, now becomes apparent.

The concept of 'outpouring' is also significant, for Steiner often pointed to love as the only 'commodity' we can give freely without ever exhausting its source. The connection of love with light is also plain. God *is* Love (1 John 4:8,16). He is also Light, (1 John 1:5), and in Christ there is Light (John 1:7–9). He is 'the true Light that lighteth every one that cometh into the world'. This is the light of consciousness that enables us not only to be aware of the spiritual world after death, but also through which our own Ego, our true Self, is illumined. When we can really and truly say, 'Not I, but Christ in me', we shall be enlightened indeed.

> I gaze into the darkness.
> In it there arises Light—
> Living Light.
> Who is this Light in the darkness?
> It is I myself in my reality.
> This reality of the 'I'
> Enters not into my earthly life;
> I am but a picture of it.
> But I shall find it again,
> When, with good will for the Spirit,
> I shall have passed through the Gate of Death.[20]

5.

What Happens After We Die?

Death is precisely the proof that in reality there is no death, that it is an illusion. If we were unable to die we could never experience a spiritual ego; for we owe the possibility of experiencing a spiritual ego to the fact that we can die physically.[1]

Experiencing kamaloka

The moment of death, Rudolf Steiner observed, is marked by the 'releasing' of our soul-spiritual principles: 'Generally speaking, it must be said: it is not the soul and spirit that forsake the body, but they are set free by the body.' Later, '...the soul will set the spirit free to pass into the higher, spiritual world...'[2] During the first three or four days the etheric body, which carries all our memories, disengages itself from the physical-material body, and it is during this period that the so-called 'life-tableau' is experienced. Briefly, this involves a panoramic survey which consists in recalling vivid memory-pictures of all the important and significant events that marked our life which has now ended. Immediately following this we embark upon a period commonly known as kamaloka, thereafter to progress through the regions of the soul world and then the spiritual world proper. All three stages are characterized by a kind of cathartic self-examination procedure from which we learn, and by which we are enabled to plan our next incarnation.

People who die young, perhaps below the age of 35, take with them into the spiritual world a considerable proportion of unused soul-spiritual forces, and these serve to strengthen them. Those who are very old when they die will have used up practically all their life-forces, but ideally this is compensated for by the accumulation of wisdom and spirituality in general over the years, assuming of course that they have not passed most of their time in idle amusement and trivial pastimes. However, gradual but inexorable destruction of our physical-material body takes place throughout our lifetime, whether through work or play, for if we could not destroy it, contended Steiner, we could never attain to perfection.

When we arrive in the spiritual world we are in a very real sense faced with what we ourselves created while on Earth. After a few days during which our life-tableau passes before us in retrospective order, we experience what is commonly referred to as being in kamaloka. During this period we hold another retrospective review of our past earthly life, but what forms the content of that review is actually the substance of what we have unconsciously thought and investigated during the time we spent asleep during our earthly lifetime. Night-time recollection of what went on during each day is total and entire; nothing is overlooked or forgotten. The length of time each individual spends in kamaloka can, in general, be calculated by reference to the sum of the hours spent in sleep, which amounts to approximately one-third of the total length of our Earthly life. Hence, the time spent in kamaloka in the case of a person who died at the age of 60 will probably be about 20 years, and 30 years if someone had died aged 90. Accordingly, children who die young spend only a few years in these circumstances.

During kamaloka we experience an intense longing in our now disembodied souls to remove everything which retards our spiritual advancement, and thus the foundations for our future karma are laid. We incorporate into our souls the forces that we must generate between death and rebirth for bringing about in our next incarnation that pattern of life experiences which we regard as right and appropriate. In other words, we develop the power of making recompense for our moral misdeeds—those things we ought not to have done, but did them nevertheless. But invariably, out of the negative develops the positive. The pain we caused another person to suffer, we ourselves now feel; every wrong we did gives rise to a strong urge in us for it to be righted. Anything in the way of 'sham', anything that is not authentic, cannot exist in this ambience. Only what is in agreement with what is true, just and morally correct can exist in the supersensible worlds of soul and spirit. At the same time, any notion of petty moralizing here can be dismissed. For the underlying ideal is that of justice or righteousness in the true sense of these terms, and *we* are in very deed our own judges.

While living our earthly lives, we may well be able to turn our energies to alleviating the pains and distresses of our fellow human beings wherever they may be, and perhaps unknown to us personally. Most people appreciate that such acts of benevolence and fellow-feeling are best made freely, without thought for reward, for in kamaloka we come to see that deeds of good will accorded our neighbours do not automatically put us, as it were, 'in credit in heaven'. We do well if we regard all monetary and other assistance purely as gifts to the world. Conversely, everything that comes to us in the way of pleasure and enjoyment has in no way been 'deserved' by us; rather, it is a gift of grace. It could be a mistake to imagine that the main purpose of our being on the Earth is for 'the pursuit of happiness', for many have learned that in the last resort mere pleasure is deeply unsatisfying.

When the period in kamaloka has been completed, we pass on through the seven states or regions of the soul world and then those of the spirit world proper, as will be described in due course. During all these stages we are obliged to face up to the fact that we are necessarily subject to, and responsible for, the events of our doing that occurred in our previous earthly life. Hence, in a very real sense, we exist in a domain of our own devising. It is important to bear in mind that in the spiritual world we perceive only what appertains to us, and this by virtue of the faculties of feeling and willing attaching to us during our previous embodiment, and which we still retain.

Thus the soul, having departed from all things terrestrial, now finds itself in an environment wherein soul-forces are pre-eminent. During our previous lifetime our soul was influenced by both the spirit 'above' and the body 'below', and served as intermediary between these two principles. Therefore, when our corporeal nature has been laid aside, our soul can have connections only with our spirit. This is not to say, however, that the impressions made during our earthly sojourn do not remain in the soul, for they certainly do. All the desires which were bodily in origin still remain, including every kind of addiction, dependence or habit. The soul is left with cravings which cannot be stilled for the simple reason that it does not have access to a physical body with which to satisfy such desires. All this has to be so, for the soul must shake off everything to do with its former existence that depended on the earthly body and the sensations enjoyed by means of it.

During our sojourn in the spiritual world we encounter the workings of the principle of reversal again and again. Those people who, while on the physical plane, exhibited a marked love of ease may now be obliged to undergo the disagreeable experience of making strenuous efforts of will. On the other hand, if our destiny had decreed that we were ill while on earth, then during our time in kamaloka we experience its opposite in terms of feeling—that is to say, a sensation of health and well-being in direct proportion to the pain and discomfort of our periods of sickness or infirmity.[3]

The seven regions of the soul world

It is important to bear in mind in what follows that the various 'regions' or 'stages' referred to are not arranged as it were one above the other, but rather interpenetrate and thus co-exist. The first stage or region of the soul world is not for nothing called 'the region of burning desire'. Its parallel in religious terms is called purgatory by the Roman Catholic Church, and hell by others. In the spiritual world all evil that we have brought about necessitates our facing its opposite quality of good, and this constitutes a kind of punishment, or 'cleansing fire', which we bring upon ourselves on account of our own immoral deeds. For example, any lies that we told during our earthly lives invoke the opposite state of affairs, namely, the truth, and this torments or 'burns' us; similarly, deceitful or trea-cherous behaviour invokes the positive desire to make amends in some way.

This is the stage at which our coarser and more selfish wishes, yearnings and cravings are purged, when the soul is bound to experience deprivation and perhaps distress, as well as frustration and disappointment. However, it is important to realize that it is the soul itself that yearns to the point of *demanding* of itself that it suffer such deprivations and denials, to experience the necessary counterbalance to our freely chosen earthly deeds.[4] So there is clearly nothing vengeful or malicious in this process, as all punitive measures are necessarily self-inflicted.

The second region is that which Steiner called *Mobile Sensitivity*, where a balancing out of the soul's sympathies and antipathies leads to a state of equilibrium. All attraction for that which was trivial during earthly life, particularly those pursuits which imparted illusions of grandeur or self-importance in the realms of what, in terms of spiritual advancement, could be considered empty and profitless, all this of necessity dies away. Fame, riches, public acclaim or adulation accorded as the result of achievements which are inconsequential in terms of progress along the path to perfection are seen for what they really were—essentially pointless and worthless. Gradually, all unfulfilled desires become extinct, and all sympathy towards them fades and disappears. Conversely, feelings of antipathy are generated towards all such 'glittering prizes', whereby everything that has been achieved that did not contribute to the welfare of our spiritual nature turns to ashes.

In the third region, that of *Wishes,* any remaining unfulfilled ambitions, dreams, desires and longings to which the soul clings in what may be construed as sympathetic or attractive aspirations are purged away sooner or later, according to the degree of attachment to these. It becomes patently clear that there is absolutely no possibility of their being realized, and so they are abandoned.

The soul passes on to the fourth stage or region, that of *Liking and Disliking.* Here a kind of plateau is reached, where the soul experiences a certain flatness or emptiness brought about by feelings of disillusionment concerning the previous desires it enjoyed through its now cast-off physical body which was formerly used to satisfy them. Feelings of being lonely and forsaken now overcome the soul, and what Rudolf Steiner termed 'recognition that the true human being does not lie in the physical' gradually dawns. This acceptance of the truth that human beings are primarily spiritual in nature, and only secondarily physical-material in nature, marks the stage at which the soul is ready to 'pour itself with full sympathy into the common soul world'.[5]

The fifth region in the soul world is that which Steiner describes as *Soul Light*, and is characterized by the extinguishing in the soul of what could be described as excessive delight and enjoyment of earthly nature without adequate appreciation of the spiritual forces behind it. Sightseeing for the sake of it, and current tendencies of cuddly sentimentality towards animals are examples of this unreflective admiration for nature.

Superfluous sensations provided for entertainment, pleasure and 'thrills' by artificial means which frequently reach 'sensory overload' proportions, such as firework displays, flashing lights and lasers, extraneous visual, musical and other effects of a superficial nature also come into this category. Excessive indulgence in religious practices characteristic of certain charismatic movements could be included, together with all excesses associated with over-indulgence in emotions based on sensory stimulation and excitation which give rise to feelings of rapturous bliss, ecstasy, euphoria and suchlike.

Eventually, the soul realizes that its propensities must be directed elsewhere, and this leads it on to the sixth region, which Steiner calls that of *Active Soul Force*. This represents the stage at which the soul is purged of any purely egotistical pleasure, pride or self-satisfaction in what it had achieved on earth, even if the achievements were of value or merit in the fields of art, science, religion or in whatever field of human endeavour.

The seventh region is that of *Soul Life*, in which the individuality is freed from the last vestiges of attachment to the sensuous physical realm. This is the stage at which even convinced materialists come to the realization that matter is indeed that in which the spiritual is perpetually at work, and is not entirely self-existent. With these last trials, the soul has now completed its earthly tasks and becomes utterly assimilated into the soul world, thus allowing the spirit-filled ego to be set free into the spirit-world proper to which it truly belongs.

Thus the soul passes through the various regions or stages of purification, and at last it has freed itself from every earthly influence. The soul remains at each stage for whatever length of time is necessary, willing to 'suffer' until a particular trait is completely extinguished. In every one of these seven stages we gradually come to the realization of what in our nature has to be purged; and this equates to what we learn to be hindrances on our path to perfection. Naturally, what we recognize as being helpful in this respect is retained. Only then is it able to pass on to the next stage, until finally the soul is able to release the spirit into the spirit-world, where it will remain until it is ripe for a new bodily existence.[6]

Progression through the spiritual regions

The urge to learn about our earthly environment, to understand it and make sense of it, is rooted deep in human nature. We are living in an age when science and its findings surround us on all sides. Scientists see it as their task to ask questions of the natural world, and every aspect of modern life shows us the results of their patient and diligent research. However, when we find ourselves in the spiritual world after death, we are surrounded by freely available wisdom. Yet again the principle of reversal manifests itself, for in these realms it is the spiritual beings who ask the questions. We are as it were continually pestered by them to supply out of ourselves the ability to answer these questions, and we find that we cannot do this if we have worked only for intellectual knowledge during our life on earth rather than for the insights of genuine wisdom. This means that we have to pass on if we cannot provide answers required by the spiritual beings, but at the same time we generate, albeit unconsciously, the intention of creating opportunities in our next incarnation designed to rectify the situation.

Thinking certainly is a spiritual *activity* which is made possible but at the same time is limited by material considerations. The challenge is to transcend the limitations that matter, by very reason of our apprehension of it by our bodily senses, imposes on our everyday thinking. In this connection it is worth reporting that Rudolf Steiner, himself trained in the science of his day, contended that scientists will never fully understand matter until they come to realize that in matter spirit is continuously at work.

The limitations of language, with its conventions of grammar and other rules, are necessary for clarity of expression and understanding, but at the same time they bestow a certain rigidity on the concepts we employ when we think. Were this not so, we should not be able to handle our ideas at all, much less construct theories, hypotheses and so on. But there seems to be a growing need nowadays for readers and hearers to divine what is meant when the language employed is inadequate or faulty. (For example, guess what is actually meant when someone says, 'She likes him better than me,' and ponder this extract from an examination board report: 'Some candidates lost unnecessary marks because they did not read the questions properly.') Clarity of thinking is always paramount, and clarity of expression more so. Furthermore, if our feelings and our will-power are also adequately exercised and engaged with effectual thinking during our Earthly lives, we generate creative power and the ability to work from out of ourselves with initiative and force while in the spiritual realms.

The physical-material world provides us with countless opportunities for our *will* to be active, using the body to accomplish deeds. The realms of the human soul are those in which our *feelings* and emotions are expressed. The domain proper to the spirit is that of *thinking*; it is in effect a thought-world. Rudolf Steiner often mentioned how very difficult it is to describe supersensory beings and entities, and explain their functions and their deeds, in ideas or concepts that are usually employed in the dense world of material things. Thus, by very reason of our constitution, spiritual beings and events are hidden from us. The very fact that we have to rely so heavily on our bodily senses virtually denies us access to the realms of soul and spirit. While on Earth we have direct experience of the material world, which constantly clamours for our attention, so that it is difficult for our thoughts to be much occupied with the concerns of the supersensory worlds.

Perception in the spiritual realms is largely a matter of becoming aware of thoughts, both of human origin and those of the spiritual hierarchies above us. The thoughts we fashion by means of our brain are mere shadows compared with the thought-forms that live as actual beings in the spiritual worlds, and many people have difficulty in grasping the fact that thoughts exist in a way that is as real as the most solid of objects.

The seven regions of the spirit world

The spirit world, like the soul world, comprises seven regions or stages, also co-existent and interpenetrating, through which the human spirit progresses, to remain in these purely spiritual realms until the time is appropriate for rebirth. Paradoxically, the spirit-filled human ego, itself indestructible and incorruptible, is able to evolve or unfold only in an environment that is physical-material in nature. We are not able to make any progress in the spiritual sense while we are in the spiritual worlds themselves. We are obliged to take on a new soul and body on the Earth, there to live among those who incarnate at the same time and become our relations, friends, enemies, and others with whom our destinies are entwined.

By reason of these associations, and the various circumstances in which they work themselves out, each individual is able to contribute to the history of the peoples of the Earth. In consequence, the Earth itself is subject over the millennia to the thoughts, feelings and ultimately the deeds of succeeding generations, which inevitably bear the stamp of every individual and have their origin in the spiritual nature of every person involved. It is by such means that whole civilizations progress and retrogress, and the whole human race is *educated,* for each member of it has to spend time in the soul and spiritual realms, there to undergo any necessary 'correction' in the interests of spiritual advancement. Thus it comes about that the spiritual is enabled to reach down into the physical-material, and the earthly to reach up into the heavenly.

The first region of the spiritual realms proper is that in which individualities are surrounded by the corresponding 'thought-models' or spiritual archetypes of earthly things. Each spirit-filled ego perceives itself to be a spirit among spirits, and these as real as we regard material objects on earth as real. Thoughts here are actual beings, perpetually and creatively constructive and actively mobile. Steiner describes the archetypes as 'master builders of all that comes into being in the physical and soul worlds', characterizing *archetype* as follows:

> In this world are to be seen, first, the spiritual arche-types of all things and beings which are present in the physical and soul worlds. Imagine the picture of a painter existing in his mind before it is painted. This gives an analogy to what is meant by the expression *archetype*. It does not concern us here that the painter has perhaps not had such an archetype in his mind before he paints; and that it only gradually develops and becomes complete during the execution of the picture. In the real world of spirit there exist such archetypes for all things, and the physical things and beings are copies of these archetypes.[7]

In this region the archetypes of material, earthly objects, including those of the human body, are regarded as a unity. At first the notion of separateness of our own bodily con-stitution persists, but gradually the conviction forms that we in our essential nature really do belong to the spiritual worlds. It is at this stage that we find again those with whom we had significant dealings in our previous life, and in a very real sense continue to live with them as a spirit among spirits.

In the second region, which Steiner describes as containing the archetypes of life, we find ourselves living in a common environment with those with whom we had shared our religious feelings of devotion, reverence and worship. The real value of religion, observed Steiner, is that we are obliged to think about things that have no direct representation in the sense-world. Such ideas cannot work directly during life, but after death serve to strengthen our soul-forces of feeling and willing.[8] We experience a strong feeling of community and fellowship at this stage, and draw strength from having shared convictions which are regarded as religious in nature.

The third region accommodates the archetypes of the soul world and all that this signifies in terms of surging feelings and profound emotions. Sensitive reactions to the needs of others while on earth, and deeds of altruism and self-denial find their rewards here. Just as all life forms a unity in the second region, in the third region all longings and wishes, all likes and dislikes form a unity. Rudolf Steiner pointed out that the first three states experienced by us in the world of spirit correspond in general terms to solid matter, all that is fluid or liquid, and to that of an airy nature respectively. It is no coincidence that there appears to be a connection between these three states and our three lower members, namely, physical body, etheric body and astral body. These have to do with the archetypal principles of Earth, Water and Air, and it comes as no surprise to learn that the fourth region of the spirit world contains all that has to do in the ideal sense with Fire—in other words, spirit proper.

This means that in the fourth region is found everything

to do with human culture. All archetypes to do with the expansion and development of thinking are to be found here, including those embracing the arts, sciences and technological inventions of all kinds, as well as cultural enterprises.

As can be seen from all this, something of our Earthly ways and culture still clings to us throughout our experience of the fourth region, and it is only at the fifth state that we become completely free of all previous influences and their effects. For the very first time our ego, purely spiritual in nature, is released to expand in all directions. Now comes the opportunity to begin afresh, and prepare for our future incarnation. We examine our intentions, purposes and objectives, and plan for future possibilities for spiritual advancement as well as their means of implementation.

According to the strength and maturity of our capacities for compassionate, altruistic love and will to action, we draw forth from our soul the necessary strength for its creative powers to be activated. The result is the awakening and gradual development of a soul-force which Rudolf Steiner described as 'soul-light'. This faculty resides in the deeper layers of our unconscious mind during Earthly life, but at death it becomes available for employment in the spiritual world as the power of illumination—as a veritable soul-light that 'streams through, shines and glitters through everything'.[9] In this manner the thoughts which abide in the environment can be grasped and understood. It is this soul-light that is lacking in those individualities who have shunned everything to do with religion or the spiritual life while on Earth, and they therefore experience darkness. Gradually, however, even those who have developed the faculty of soul-light begin to experience its waxing and waning, when periods of darkened consciousness of the soul-world alternate with periods when they are able to illuminate their surroundings. This resembles something like sleeping and waking: a time of spiritual interaction is followed by one of solitude, and these states proceed in alternate fashion.

However, such periods of solitude are by no means depressing or distressing, for they are taken up with a kind of creative reflection on all that has been experienced in the spiritual world so far, and retained as memories. The creative urge becomes stronger and ever stronger, and the spiritual apprehension dimmer and dimmer, and there gradually awakens the yearning to experience an outer world again. This creative longing develops into the power of re-experiencing our previous life, and this forms so to speak a world of our own creation within our already existing world.

At the sixth stage we are able to bring to bear all that we have acquired in the way of wisdom, true altruism and self-sacrifice; and the urge is felt to deploy these gifts for the good of humankind in general during the course of our next earthly embodiment. Being now virtually free of any influences from our previous lives, such plans are devised in an utterly dispassionate and objective manner, with only the good of our spirit-filled ego—which almost by definition means the benefit of our fellow human beings—in view. Thus we shape our own destiny with the over-whelming purpose in mind to remedy our deficiencies, faults and shortcomings. Said Steiner:

> Experiences which in the following earth life appear as a painful destiny, seen from that life—and perhaps deeply bewailed as such—are, nevertheless, the very experiences which the human being in this region of spiritland finds absolutely necessary for himself.[10]

Yet again the principle of reversal is seen to operate, for just as after death we undertake a backward review of our past life in kamaloka, so, shortly before our rebirth on the material plane, we experience a preview of the salient features of our future Earthly life. Of great significance at this stage is the ability for us to gain access to divine wisdom, of which we are granted instant and genuine understanding. We live in the presence of exalted and powerful spiritual beings from whom help may be sought, and a sense of earnest willingness to fulfil our individual destiny within a harmonious world order remains paramount throughout.

During Earthly life, if we are to attain to the wisdom of the world, it requires of us much effort and mental labour. However in the spiritual world after death we are surrounded by an abundance of wisdom, just as we are surrounded by Nature in the material world. Our task is now to generate from this wisdom the forces we shall need for a future life on earth, that is to say, produce what is material out of what is essentially spiritual. We shall be able to do this only if we were able in our previous life to recognize something of a spiritual nature behind the materiality of our environment. A convinced materialist, for example, will find it very difficult at this stage to avoid being overwhelmed by the experience.[11]

Everything reaches its culmination in the seventh and last region, for we have now lived in and traversed the three spheres of existence, namely, the *physical-material world* of minerals, plants, animals and fellow humans, the *world of soul* with its seven states, and finally the *realms of spirit*. It is only after experiencing all that the regions of the soul and spiritual worlds have to offer that the 'thirst for Earthly existence' sets in. We begin to yearn for the opportunities to gain more self-knowledge and make further progress on the path to perfection, which are only possible on Earth.

The Midnight Hour of Existence

We have now become able to see ourselves as we really are, and to recognize our own particular 'spiritual seeds', which will be sown into these three worlds in order that our individual tasks may be fulfilled. In our new life these 'spiritual seeds' will remain in the unattainable depths of our consciousness, from there to influence our actions and behaviour. Irrespective of our almost certain objections to the blows of fate that we ourselves will have induced and engineered in the course of our new Earthly existence, our higher Self, our true Ego, knows that this is what is necessary for our eternal welfare.

All the experiences so far described occupy the first half of the whole time between death and rebirth. Now we are approaching the midpoint of our sojourn in the spiritual world, that which Rudolf Steiner called the Midnight Hour of Existence. This is the time when we experience special feelings of solitude, of inner intensity, when our interaction and association with the spiritland has reached its lowest level. The longing arises for re-embodiment in a physical environment, and in doing so we take into account all that our experiences while in the spiritual world have brought to us along the lines already discussed.

We come to realize that much of that which gave us bodily pleasure and enjoyment delivered little in the way of moral progress, whereas what we experienced during our previous incarnation as pain and woe actually gave us moral strength, and was to be valued for this reason. We are also able to anticipate what it is necessary to do in order to compensate for our misdeeds in previous lives. Our will is fired to accomplish deeds which are of value to humankind and the Earthly world in various ways according to our destiny, and attempt to determine our actions in ways appropriate to our deepest aspirations.

Sustaining confidence in the future

Rudolf Steiner often spoke about the importance of our harbouring feelings of gratitude for everything with which we are favoured, and indeed for the very gift of life itself.[12] Such an attitude of thankfulness should be extended to include unpleasant experiences as well, even the blows that destiny deals us, including the death of dear ones, sickness, infirmity and so on, although such notions may be difficult to accept at first.

But it is usually the case that out of what is seemingly bad eventually comes good, and those of us who find themselves bereaved, in spite of our sadness and sorrow, gradually adjust to whatever circumstances obtain. As time goes on, our acceptance of these may well give rise to feelings, perhaps vague and confused to start with, that the changes that have occurred are part of an overall pattern in terms of destiny. We come to cherish memories of those dear to us who have died, and to be thankful for having been able to share past joys and pleasures with them, and for the recollections of significant events experienced together. It is less distressing to do this than wistfully and longingly to wish them back. Moreover, this kind of response to bereavement creates very real hindrances to any attempts we make to forge links with those who have died with whom we wish to remain in contact, and with whom communication is possible to achieve, as discussed earlier. Gradually a positive outlook will become easier to foster, and we may come to realize that in the first place we have not really lost our loved ones, and secondly, that the related circumstances and events were indeed brought about by them in accordance with the laws of karma or self-created destiny. If all this is grasped properly we shall be ready to establish the kind of 'meeting-ground' mentioned earlier in terms of commonality of thought-content.

Naturally, this attitude of being grateful for all that we are favoured means just that—all of life's experiences must be included, and if we are able to extend this general feeling of sharing with the whole world, then so much the better. From this standpoint of calm acceptance of our karma, we are more and more able to develop a mood of confidence in life, and also faith in the universe at large. Undoubtedly, the feeling that life has meaning and purpose is of considerable advantage, and confidence in the reality that we truly are 'captains of our soul, and masters of our fate' will intensify.[13] It should not be difficult to appreciate that the two factors Rudolf Steiner stressed, and which we have discussed, namely, gratitude for all that with which we have been favoured and an attitude of trust in the universe, complement and supplement each other.[14] Similarly, the feelings of unity with our loved ones who have died, which are fostered by the cultivation of common thought-content, give rise to hopes for future spiritual betterment on the part of both us and them. We are therefore well placed for realizing that our bereavement can, if we allow it, bring about the development and enhancement of progress on the path to perfection for our dear departed as well as ourselves.

We must eradicate from the soul all fear and terror of what comes towards mankind out of the future. We must look forward with absolute equanimity to all that may come, and we must think only, that whatever comes is given to us by a world-direction full of wisdom. It is part of what we must learn in this age, namely, to live out of pure trust, without any security in existence; trust in the ever-present help of the spiritual world. Truly, nothing else will do if our courage is not to fail us. Let us discipline our will, and let us seek the awakening from within ourselves, every morning and every evening.

Rudolf Steiner[15]

Notes and References

All references are to works by Rudolf Steiner, unless otherwise indicated. Steiner's work is available in English translation from Rudolf Steiner Press, London, and Anthroposophic Press, New York.

Quotation on Title Page: *Truth-Wrought Words*, Anthroposophic Press, p. 97.

Chapter 1. Our Spiritual Roots (pages 1–13)

1. *Verses and Meditations*, Rudolf Steiner Press, p. 199.
2. Memorial Speech, Dornach, 29 June 1923, *Life Beyond Death*, chapter 10, Rudolf Steiner Press, 1995.
3. Cloos, W., *The Living Earth*, Lanthorn Press, 1977.
4. *Study of Man*, Rudolf Steiner Press, p. 32; *The Renewal of Education*, Rudolf Steiner Press, p. 20.
5. *A Theory of Knowledge Implicit in Goethe's World-Conception*, Rudolf Steiner Press. See also Chapter 3.

Chapter 2. The Complexities of Human Nature (pages 15–29)

1. *Verses and Meditations*, Rudolf Steiner Press, p. 107.
2. *Theosophy*, Anthroposophical Publishing Co, 1946, Chapter 1.
3. *Theosophy*, pp. 6–8; *Man as a Being of Sense and Perception*, Steiner Book Centre, 1981, *passim*; also *Between Death and Rebirth*, Rudolf Steiner Press, for further reading concerning cosmic aspects.

4. For further discussion, see Poppelbaum, E., *Man and Animal: Their Essential Difference*, Anthroposophical Publishing Co, 1931; and Lehrs, E., *Man or Matter*, Faber & Faber, 1951, Rudolf Steiner Press, 1996.

Chapter 3. How Do We Experience Immortality? (pages 31–51)

1. Steiner, R., *Life Beyond Death*, Rudolf Steiner Press, 1995, p. 208f.
2. ITV Programme *Strange but True?*, 18 October 1996. See also Morse, M., *Transformed by the Light*, Piatkus, 1995.
3. Books by Dr E. Kübler-Ross include: *Living with Death and Dying; On Children and Death; On Death and Dying*; and *Questions and Answers on Death and Dying*.
4. *Life Beyond Death*, p. 168.
5. *At the Gates of Spiritual Science*, Lecture 3; *Theosophy* p. 138.
6. *Life Beyond Death*, p. 172.
7. *The Forming of Destiny and the Life After Death*, Lecture 1, Berlin, 16 November 1915, Anthroposophical Publishing Company, 1927.
8. *Verses and Meditations*, p. 209.
9. *The Dead are with Us*, 10 February 1918.
10. *Truth-Wrought Words*, Rudolf Steiner Press, p. 13.
11. *Life Between Death and Rebirth*, p. 272.
12. *Christ and the Human Soul*, Lecture 1, Norrköping, 12 July 1914.
13. Ibid.
14. *Verses and Meditations*, p. 210.

Chapter 4. Achieving Communion with Those Who Have Died (pages 53–73)

1. *Verses and Meditations*, p. 217.
2. *The Forming of Destiny and Life after Death*, Lecture 2, Berlin, 18 November 1915.
3. *The Dead are with Us*, 10 February 1918.

4. *Earthly Life and Cosmic Death*, Lecture 4, Berlin, 5 March 1915.

5. *The Forming of Destiny and Life after Death*, Lecture 4, Berlin, 7 December 1915.

6. Ibid.

7. *Links Between the Living and the Dead*, Rudolf Steiner Press, 1973, pp. 8–28.

8. *Life beyond Death*, p. 154.

9. Ibid., p. 227.

10. *Truth-Wrought Words*, p. 92.

11. *How to Know Higher Worlds*, Chapter 1.

12. See *How to Know Higher Worlds*; *Occult Science—an Outline*; *Theosophy*; *A Road to Self Knowledge*; *The Threshold of the Spiritual World*; *Stages of Higher Knowledge*; *Verses and Meditations*; *Truth-Wrought Words*.

13. *Guidance in Esoteric Training*, p. 77.

14. 'The Establishment of Mutual Relations Between the Living and the Dead', 20 February 1913, in *Occult Research into Life Between Death and a New Birth*, Anthroposophic Press, 1949.

15. *Guidance in Esoteric Training*, p. 79.

16. *The Inner Nature of Man and the Life after Death*, Lecture 3, Rudolf Steiner Press 1994.

17. *Love and Its Meaning in the World*, Rudolf Steiner Press.

18. *Verses and Meditations*, p. 213.

19. *Guidance in Esoteric Training*, pp. 48–49.

20. *Truth-Wrought Words*, p. 65.

Chapter 5. What Happens After We Die? (pages 75–93)

1. *The Forming of Destiny and Life after Death*, Lecture 1, Berlin, 16 November 1915.

2. *Theosophy*, p. 126ff.

3. *The Inner Nature of Man and Life after Death*, Lecture 4.

4. *Theosophy*, p 135.

5. Ibid., p. 137.

6. Ibid., p. 156.
7. Ibid., p. 145ff.
8. *The Inner Nature of Man and Life after Death*, Lecture 3.
9. Ibid., Lecture 5.
10. *Theosophy*, p. 175ff.
11. *The Inner Nature of Man and Life after Death*, Lecture 4.
12. *Earthly Death and Cosmic Life*, Lecture 7.
13. For further discussion see Childs, G., *From Birthlessness to Deathlessness*, Fire Tree Press, 1996, p. 158 and *passim*.
14. *Earthly Death and Cosmic Life*, Lecture 7.
15. This quotation is said to be from an unpublished lecture by Rudolf Steiner given on 27 November 1910 in Bremen. (There are no verbatim shorthand reports of the lecture, and the reports that exist are fragmentary.)

Rudolf Steiner
LIFE BEYOND DEATH

While western humanity has conquered the outer world with the aid of technology and natural science, the mysterious question of death is still largely shrouded in fear, and remains an insoluble riddle.

From his own highly-developed clairvoyance, Rudolf Steiner was able spiritually to research the question of what happens to human beings after their physical bodies pass away. Life continues beyond death, he affirms in these astonishing lectures, and the human being awakens to a new higher reality, where the soul begins a great journey to the farthest expanses of the cosmos. When the discarnated soul has been purified and prepared, it then begins the descent into a new physical body for a new incarnation.

Rudolf Steiner suggests that one of the most important tasks for our present civilisation is to re-establish living connections with those who have died. He gives instructions as to how this can be done, and also describes how the dead can be of help to us in our lives on earth.

RUDOLF STEINER PRESS
256pp; ISBN 1 85584 017 0; £11.95